FUN BIBLE TRIVIA

2

Tamela Hancock Murray

BARBOUR
PUBLISHING, INC.
Uhrichsville, Ohio

Scripture taken from the Good News Bible in Today's English Version copyright © 1992 by American Bible Society. Used by permission.

Published by Barbour Publishing, Inc., P.O. Box 719, Uhrichsville, Ohio 44683   http://www.barbourbooks.com

Member of the
Evangelical Christian
Publishers Association

Printed in the United States of America.

FUN
BIBLE
TRIVIA

THE CRUISE OF A LIFETIME

1. You can find the story of Noah's ark in the Book of
   a. Genesis.
   b. Revelation.
   c. The Love Boat.
   d. Noah.

2. True or False: In Noah's time, God was pleased with his creation.

3. In Noah's time, God decided he would
   a. rain manna on all the people.
   b. destroy all the people, animals, and birds he had created.
   c. give everyone a computer for school.
   d. send missionaries to give everyone a New Testament Bible.

4. True or False: Noah was the only good man living in his time.

5. How many sons did Noah have?

6. Can you name Noah's sons? Hint: One of them has the same name as a famous Virginia meat product.

7. Did you know that God told Noah to take seven pairs of each type of bird with him into the ark (Genesis 7:3)? He also told Noah to take one pair of each ritually unclean animal and seven pairs of each ritually clean animal (Genesis 7:2).

8. What is a ritually clean beast?

9. When the flood started Noah was
   a. 6 years old.   c. 600 years old.
   b. 60 years old.   d. 666 years old.

10. How long did it rain?

11. Did you know that the water rose until it was about twenty-five feet over the highest mountains? (Genesis 7:20).

12. Noah could see the mountain tops after
    a. 7 1/2 months.
    b. 10 months.
    c. 7 days.
    d. 40 days and 40 nights.

13. Did you know that, after the flood, the water did not start going down for 150 days?

14. True or False: The first bird Noah sent out from the ark was a dove.

15. After the second time out, the dove brought Noah
    a. an Amy Grant CD.
    b. another dove.
    c. a McDonald's Happy Meal.
    d. an olive branch.

16. True or False: Noah was 601 years old when he and his family got out of the ark.

17. After God saved Noah's family from the flood, Noah
    a. opened Noah's Yacht Club.
    b. made a golden calf.
    c. built an altar to God and made sacrifices upon it.
    d. learned to swim.

18. True or False: God promised not to destroy the earth by flood again.

19. What caused God to make such a promise?

20. What do we often see after rainfall that reminds us of God's promise to Noah?

A TOWERING PROBLEM

1. Where in the Bible can you find the story of the Tower of Babel?

2. True or False:
   When the people first started building the Tower of Babel, they all spoke the same language.

3. The people who built the tower spoke
   a. Latin.
   b. Hebrew.
   c. French and Spanish.
   d. an unspecified language.

4. Did you know that the Tower of Babel was built in Babylonia? The Bible says the people had settled on a plain in Shinar, which was in ancient Babylonia (Genesis 11:2).

5. The tower was built of
   a. wood.   c. brick.
   b. stone.   d. steel.

6. True or False: The people were building a city as well as a tower.

7. The people wanted a tower that would
   a. let them see the Atlantic Ocean.
   b. be three feet taller than The Empire State Building.
   c. make a suitable home for Rapunzel.
   d. reach to heaven.

8. True or False: God was happy when He saw the tower.

9. When He saw the tower, God
   a. gave the people a golden calf.
   b. asked Satan to loan the builders pitchforks to help them finish it.
   c. told the workmen how to make better bricks.
   d. made the people all speak different languages so they couldn't finish the work.

10. Why is the story of the Tower of Babel important?

GOD'S PROMISE
TO ABRAHAM

1. Did you know that the story of Abraham is found in the book of Genesis?

2. In which chapter can you find the story of God's promise to Abraham?

3. True or False: Abraham was named Abram before God changed his name.

4. How old was Abraham when God appeared to him?

5. God told Abraham to
   a. build an ark.
   b. become Jesus' disciple.
   c. obey Him.
   d. make a movie called *The Ten Commandments*.

6. When Abraham saw God, he
   a. told God he was afraid.
   b. bowed down, touching his face to the ground.
   c. built an altar.
   d. asked Him for a son.

7. God wanted to make a covenant with Abraham. What is a covenant?

8. True or False: God promised Abraham he would have many descendants.

9. A descendant is
   a. a member of a future generation.
   b. an ancestor.
   c. a person walking down a staircase.
   d. an airplane going down in the sky.

10. God also promised Abraham
    a. great riches.
    b. a chariot and seven swift horses.
    c. a coat of many colors.
    d. the land of Canaan.

11. True or False: God plans for His covenant with Abraham to last forever.

12. God gave Abram the name "Abraham" because
    a. it fit better with the song "Father Abraham."
    b. it was easier to spell.
    c. Abraham was to be the father of many nations.
    d. He wanted to name him after Abraham Lincoln.

13. True or False: God said that some of Abraham's descendants would be kings.

14. True or False: As part of the covenant, God wanted Abraham and his descendants to worship Him.

15. God changed the name of Abraham's wife. Do you remember what Sarah's name was before God changed it?

16. God promised Sarah she would
    a. never have to work again.
    b. live in a tent until she was ninety.
    c. have a baby.
    d. be the first woman president of the United States.

17. When God promised Abraham that his wife Sarah would have a baby, Abraham
    a. bowed down to God.
    b. laughed.
    c. sang God a psalm.
    d. wrote the Pentateuch.

18. Which did God promise Sarah, a baby boy, or a baby girl?

19. Abraham was surprised by God's promise because Sarah
    a. had vowed never to have children.
    b. was CEO of a large company and had no time for kids.
    c. was ninety years old, which is usually too old to have a baby.
    d. already had thirteen boys.

20. How old was Abraham when God promised him that Sarah would  bear a baby?

21. Did you know that Abraham suggested another heir? He told God that his son Ishmael could be his heir (Genesis 17:18).

22. An heir is
    a. a person with too much hair.
    b. an honest mistake.
    c. a person who receives an inheritance.
    d. an airhead.

23. True or False: God agreed with Abraham that Ishmael should be Abraham's heir.

24. True or False: All males in Abraham's household were required to take a physical mark to show they were in covenant with God.

25. How do you think Abraham's covenant with God affects you today?

THE TEN COMMANDMENTS

1. Did you know that the Ten Commandments appear in the Bible twice? You can find them in Exodus 20:1-17 and Deuteronomy 5:1-21.

2. True or False: Exodus and Deuteronomy are both New Testament books.

3. Who wrote the first five books of the Bible?

4. Did you know that the first five books of the Bible are called the Pentateuch?

5. Can you name all five books of the Pentateuch?

6. When God issued the Ten Commandments, He was on
   a. the banks of the River Jordan.
   b. Mount Sinai.
   c. Israel's TV Channel 6.
   d. Mount Ararat.

7. Did you know that Exodus means departure?

8. When God gave them the Ten
   Commandments, the Israelites had just
   a. traveled the Information Highway.
   b. been brought out of slavery in Egypt.
   c. discovered electricity.
   d. celebrated the release of
      the movie *Star Wars*.

9. True or False: The First
   Commandment is God's
   law to worship no
   other god except Him.

10. Do you think The First
    Commandment is the most important? Why?

11. True or False: It is OK to worship statues,
    money, and other earthly goods as long as
    we attend church every Sunday.

12. What does God mean when He says not to
    take His name "in vain"?

13. God commands us to set aside one day a week to
    a. gather manna.
    b. read the Bible and only drink water all day.
    c. watch cartoons.
    d. keep holy, cease work, and remember His people's deliverance from Egypt.

14. True or False: On the Sabbath, the head of the household may rest, but everyone else should work.

15. Why did God say He wanted us to rest every seventh day?

16. Did you know that the Ten Commandments are divided into two sections? The first four tell us how to show love to God. The rest tell us how to show love to other people.

17. Think about the Sabbath. How do you show your love to God on His special day?

18. God tells us to honor our
    a. pastor.
    b. friends.
    c. father and mother.
    d. teachers and principal.

19. True or False: The Sixth Commandment tells us not to murder.

20. God's commandment not to commit adultery shows us how much God values marriage. Where does God establish the institution of marriage?

21. The Eighth Commandment tells us not to
    a. burp in public.
    b. be mean to our brothers and sisters.
    c. steal.
    d. be angry with others.

22. The King James Version of the Bible tells us that God says not to "bear false witness" against our neighbor. The New International Version says we should not give "false testimony." What do these phrases in Exodus 20:16 and Deuteronomy 5:20 mean?

23. Sometimes it is hard not to lie because the truth can hurt someone's feelings. How can you be truthful without being mean?

24. God tells us not to covet other people's possessions. That means we should not
    a. steal from our friends.
    b. destroy other people's belongings.
    c. make fun of others.
    d. wish we had our neighbor's stuff.

25. God also gave Moses other laws. Most of them can be found in the Book of
    a. Leviticus.   c. Acts.
    b. Numbers.   d. Revelation.

26. Did you know that God wrote the Ten Commandments Himself? (Deuteronomy 9:9-11).

27. The Lord wrote The Ten Commandments on
    a. sheepskin.   c. parchment.
    b. stone tablets.   d. Thursday.

28. True or False: The original copy of the Ten Commandments is on display at the Jerusalem Museum.

29. Now that you have learned about The Ten Commandments, can you name all of them?

30. Did you know that before God gave us the Ten Commandments, man's laws were often self-centered, fickle, spiteful, and unjust? God's law, established in the Ten Commandments, is uniform, fair, and just.

Joshua's Famous Battle

1. Did you know that when he was a young man, Joshua served in the tabernacle? (Exodus 33:11).

2. True or False: Moses was led by God to appoint Joshua to be his successor.

3. Did you know that Joshua is the first of the Bible's historical books? Although the first five books discuss history, they are considered part of the Pentateuch.

4. The book of Joshua begins recording what happened right after
   a. the Israelites went whitewater rafting on the Jordan River.
   b. The American Revolution.
   c. the death of Moses.
   d. the birth of Jesus.

5. Is Joshua found in the Old Testament or the New Testament?

6. Who wrote the book of Joshua?

7. God told Joshua to take the people of Israel to the land He had promised them, located across the
   a. Red Sea.
   b. Grand Canyon.
   c. Jordan River.
   d. Nile River.

8. True or False: God said the Israelites should never become discouraged because He would be with them where ever they went.

9. Joshua's spies in Jericho stayed at
   a. a Holiday Inn.
   b. a Pharisee's house.
   c. the home of a wicked woman.
   d. Mary Magdalene's house.

10. True or False: Rahab protected the spies from the men of Jericho.

11. Did you know that no one could leave or enter a city after the gate was closed at sundown? Rahab tricked the men who were chasing Joshua's spies and told them to look outside the city. Because the men were locked out after sundown, they could not harm the spies (Joshua 2:4-7).

12. Rahab hid the spies
    a. on the roof.
    b. in the wine cellar.
    c. in the bathtub.
    d. under her bed.

13. Did you know that in addition to protecting them, Rahab gave the spies valuable information? She told them that the people of Jericho were afraid of the Israelites. This gave the spies confidence that the Lord would help them conquer Jericho (Joshua 2:9 and 2:24).

14. True or False: Rahab accepted the Lord and asked the spies for mercy.

15. Why did Rahab protect the spies?

16. Did you know that God stopped the Jordan River from flowing while the Israelites crossed it into the promised land? The river was usually flooded at that time of year, so crossing it on foot would have been impossible without God's miracle. The stopping of the river also allowed the ark of the covenant to stay dry while the priests carried it (Joshua 3:14-17).

17. What was the ark of the covenant?

18. How many men crossed the plains of Jericho to fight for the Lord?

19. The Israelites no longer had manna to eat after they had
    a. been punished for watching too much TV.
    b. eaten food grown in the promised land.
    c. gotten tired of eating quail meat.
    d. sinned.

20. What was manna?

21. Did you know that God sent a divine commander to help the Israelites defeat Jericho? Although the Bible calls him a man, we know he was divine, because Joshua bowed before him and the man told Joshua to take off his shoes because he was on holy ground (Joshua 5:13-15).

22. True or False: The walls of Jericho came tumbling down after the Israelites threw rocks and stones at them.

23. Whose family was spared during the fall of Jericho?

24. All the silver, gold, bronze, and iron in Jericho was
    a. used to improve the ark of the covenant.
    b. put into the Lord's treasury.
    c. used to build the Tower of Babel.
    d. made into fancy jewelry.

25. True or False: After the fall of Jericho, Joshua became famous in the land.

DAVID FIGHTS GOLIATH

1. You can find the story of David's battle with Goliath in
   a. 1 Samuel.
   b. The Book of David.
   c. the book *Goliath: The Bigger They Are, The Harder They Fall.*
   d. Jude.

2. Did you know that Goliath of Gath was over nine feet tall? (1 Samuel 17:4).

3. True or False: Goliath was never heavily armed. He depended on his size to protect him.

4. True or False: When Goliath challenged the Israelites to send a man to fight him, many men eagerly volunteered.

5. Why did David visit the Israelites' battlefield?

6. Before he met Goliath, David
   a. was next in line to be a high priest.
   b. tended sheep.
   c. was a prince of Israel.
   d. learned to fight giants by jousting with a
      cousin.

7. Gath was located in what
   country? Hint: Goliath
   was from Gath and the
   Israelites were battling
   his country.

8. True or False: While
   David was visiting his
   brothers on the battlefield,
   Goliath challenged the
   Israelites.

9. Did you know that King Saul had promised a
   reward to the person who killed Goliath? In
   addition to money, King Saul promised his
   daughter in marriage, and the victor's father's
   family would not have to pay taxes (1 Samuel
   17:25).

10. True or False: David's brothers were sure David could easily slay Goliath.

11. When David heard the giant's challenge, he
    a. wondered how Goliath dared to defy the army of the living God.
    b. became scared and ran home.
    c. decided to videotape Goliath to show on *Real TV*.
    d. threatened to take Goliath to court for saying mean things.

12. Saul did not want David to fight Goliath because David
    a. already had plans to attend seminary.
    b. was a consultant to King Saul on how to fix Social Security.
    c. was only a boy.
    d. was an old man.

13. Did you know that King Saul gave David his own bronze helmet and coat of armor to use when fighting Goliath? (1 Samuel 17:38).

14. True or False: David convinced King Saul to let him fight Goliath by telling him that God had protected David from the lions and bears that attacked his sheep.

15. David took Saul's armor off, because
    a. the color bronze clashed with his dark hair.
    b. Saul's armor was out of style.
    c. he couldn't walk in it because he wasn't used to such cumbersome armor.
    d. his friends at the mall would make fun of him for not looking cool.

16. How many smooth stones did David pick up to battle Goliath?

17. True or False: When Goliath saw David coming to battle him, he shook with fear.

18. David told Goliath that his victory over him would prove that
    a. the pen is mightier than the sword.
    b. he had been paying attention when he watched *Terminator 2*.
    c. size means nothing.
    d. there is a God in Israel.

19. True or False: Goliath fell with the first stone David hurled at him.

20. After Goliath died, the Israelites
    a. chased the Philistines back to their own country.
    b. offered the Philistines a permanent peace treaty.
    c. slept.
    d. sang "I'm in the Lord's Army!"

ELISHA PERFORMS
MANY MIRACLES

1. True or False: Elisha was the son of the prophet Elijah.

2. You can find out about Elisha in
   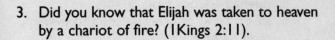
   a. I Kings.
   b. 2 Kings.
   c. Matthew.
   d. Revelation.

3. Did you know that Elijah was taken to heaven by a chariot of fire? (1Kings 2:11).

4. Can you name another godly person who was taken to heaven without dying?

5. True or False: Elisha asked for a "double portion" of Elijah's spirit.

33

6. Elisha's first miracle was
   a. making 5,000 Spamburgers from one can of Spam.
   b. dividing the Jordan. River and walking on dry land.
   c. inventing the cotton gin.
   d. getting the children of Jericho to eat broccoli soup.

7. True or False: The fifty prophets of Jericho saw the miracle and proclaimed that Elijah's power was upon Elisha.

8. In Jericho, Elisha
   a. opened a Coca Cola factory.
   b. gave a bowl of broccoli soup to every child he met.
   c. made the water pure.
   d. turned water into wine.

9. Some boys in Bethel made fun of Elisha for being
   a. a stamp collector.   c. bald.
   b. vertically challenged.   d. a dweeb.

10. Did you know that Elisha was so famous, kings asked him for advice? King Jehoshaphat of Judah, King Joram of Israel, and the King of Edom asked him how to defeat the Moabites (2 Kings 3:13).

11. The Moabites had
    a. poisoned the Jordan River.
    b. turned the Nile River red.
    c. rebelled against Israel.
    d. been involved in a junk bond scandal on Wall Street.

12. True or False: Elisha told the kings to build ditches in a dry stream bed.

13. The next day, the Moabites decided to loot the Israelites' camp because
    a. Elisha told them to.
    b. Jezebel rose from the dead and promised victory.
    c. they thought the water they saw around the camp was blood.
    d. they had promised to bring their girl-friends some jewelry.

14. What happened when the Moabites reached the Israelites' camp?

15. True or False: The Israelites conquered all of Moab until only the capital city of Kir-haraseth was left.

16. Later, a widow asked Elisha for help because she
    a. was in debt.
    b. wanted to be beautiful.
    c. wanted to find another husband.
    d. wanted him to change the school cafeteria menu from fish sticks to pizza.

17. The only item the widow had in her house was
    a. a small coin called a mite.
    b. a brass monkey.
    c. a picture of Jesus.
    d. a small jar of olive oil.

18. Describe the miracle that happened when the widow followed Elisha's instructions.

19. True or False: Because of Elisha's advice, the widow had enough money to pay off her debts, with enough left over to live on.

20. Elisha offered to put in a good word with the king for a rich woman who had been kind to him. Did she accept his offer?

21. Elisha rewarded the Shunammite woman's kindness by
    a. praising her to the king.
    b. promising her that she would have a baby.
    c. giving her permission to charge toll to people entering Jerusalem.
    d. giving her free cable television for a year.

22. The kindness that the woman had done for Elisha was
    a. giving him water at the well.
    b. buying him tickets to see WrestleFest America.
    c. setting up a room for him to stay in when he visited.
    d. washing his feet with expensive CK One perfume.

23. True or False: Years later, Elisha performed a miracle for the woman's son.

24. Elisha:
    a. brought the boy back from the dead.
    b. refused to perform a miracle.
    c. healed the boy's blindness.
    d. gave the boy wisdom so he could pass his college entrance exams.

25. Did you know that Elisha fed 100 men with twenty loaves of bread? Even though this normally would not have been enough food for so many, they all feasted and had food left over (2 Kings 4:42-44).

26. Which one of Jesus' miracles does this story make you remember?

27. True or False: Elisha purified a pot of stew that contained poisonous gourds.

28. True or False: Naaman was a respected Egyptian commander.

29. Naaman suffered from
    a. leprosy.   c. negative cash flow.
    b. the flu.   d. cowardice.

30. Who suggested that Elisha could cure Naaman?

31. Did you know that when Naaman arrived in Israel to see Elisha, he had a letter from his king, thirty thousand pieces of silver, six thousand pieces of gold, and ten changes of fine clothes? (2 Kings 5:5-6).

32. When King Jehoram of Israel saw Naaman, he thought
    a. "I'll be rich now!"
    b. "I will only ask for the silver, lest I look greedy."
    c. "I do not have the power of God! The Syrian king wants to quarrel with me."
    d. "Gross! A leper!"

33. True or False: Elisha was not afraid to try to heal Naaman. He told the king that he would prove Israel had a prophet.

34. Elisha sent his servant to tell Naaman to
    a. wash seven times in the Jordan River.
    b. sacrifice five rams.
    c. sit on a stump and say "Bobiddy Boo Boo!" three times.
    d. go to a leper colony.

35. When Naaman was told what he should do to get well, he
    a. cried.   c. was eager to proceed.
    b. was angry.   d. decided to kill Elisha.

36. True or False: Elisha's instructions caused Naaman to become even more sick.

37. After Naaman was cured, whose god did he vow to worship?

38. Did you know that Naaman asked Elisha for some of Israel's soil to take back with him to Syria? (2 Kings 5:17). At this time, people believed you could only worship a god on his own land. Today, we know the Lord can be worshipped anywhere.

39. The amount of soil Naaman took with him was
    a. a jar full.   c. a peck.
    b. a bushel.   d. two mule loads.

40. Did you know Elisha refused to accept any payment in return for curing Naaman? (2 Kings 5:16).

41. True or False: Elisha's servant ran after Naaman and asked him for money and clothes.

42. Did Naaman give the servant any gifts?

43. True or False: Elisha was happy with the servant's actions.

44. When he heard what Gehazi had done, Elisha
    a. rewarded him with half the money.
    b. complimented Gehazi on how smart he was.
    c. gave him a bigger Christmas bonus than usual for his efforts.
    d. said that Gehazi and his family would always be plagued with leprosy.

A Visit From the Queen

1. Can you find the story of the queen's visit to Solomon in the Old Testament or the New Testament?

2. The queen was from
    a. Egypt.
    b. France.
    c. Babylon.
    d. Sheba.

3. The queen visited King Solomon because
    a. she had heard of his fame.
    b. she was looking for a husband.
    c. she was hungry and heard he served great food.
    d. he had the best pinball arcade in all of Israel.

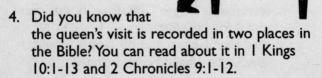

4. Did you know that the queen's visit is recorded in two places in the Bible? You can read about it in 1 Kings 10:1-13 and 2 Chronicles 9:1-12.

5. Did you know that, according to Bible scholars, the queen's country was located about twelve hundred miles from Jerusalem? Although airplanes make traveling such distances easy today, the queen had to go by camel or horseback, making the trip long and difficult.

6. True or False: The queen wanted to test Solomon with difficult questions.

7. The queen's first question was
   a. Which came first, the chicken or the egg?
   b. Where is your mine, King Solomon?
   c. Is the moon made of cheese?
   d. unknown. Her questions are not recorded in the Bible.

8. The queen was amazed by Solomon's
   a. wisdom and sacrifices to God.
   b. hair style.
   c. ability to recite the entire Bible from memory.
   d. skill at Nintendo.

9. The queen was also amazed by Solomon's
   a. willingness to live a life of poverty.
   b. allegiance to Jesus Christ.
   c. riches, palace, food, and servants.
   d. ability to read her mind and perform
      magic tricks.

10. True or False: The queen told Solomon she
    was disappointed that he didn't know as
    much as she had been told.

11. True or False: After she had spoken with
    Solomon, the queen praised the Lord.

12. If the queen did praise God, why would this
    be important?

13. Did you know that the queen gave Solomon
    666 talents of gold, and many spices and jew-
    els? (1 Kings 10:9 and 2 Chronicles 9:10).

14. If one talent weighs seventy-five
    pounds, how many pounds of
    gold did the Queen of Sheba
    give to Solomon?

NEHEMIAH BUILDS A WALL

1. Can you find the book of Nehemiah in the Old Testament or the New Testament?

2. Who wrote the book of Nehemiah?

3. Did you know that the book of Nehemiah was written about 430 BC?

4. In Nehemiah's time, the Jews in Jerusalem were
   a. rich.
   b. happy.
   c. suffering.
   d. in charge of Jerusalem's stock exchange.

5. True or False: When the book of Nehemiah begins, the walls of Jerusalem have just been built.

6. True or False: Nehemiah asked the Lord to allow the king to have mercy on him.

7. When he heard about the people's plight, Nehemiah
   a. wept and prayed to God.
   b. ran away to Tarsus.
   c. recommended psychotherapy.
   d. fled and ended up in the belly of a fish.

8. Nehemiah was the king's

   a. food taster.
   b. cup bearer.
   c. jester.
   d. spin doctor.

9. King Artaxerxes noticed that Nehemiah
   a. had spilled wine on the palace's white carpet.
   b. looked sad.
   c. had the ability to interpret dreams.
   d. had written him a message on the wall.

10. Nehemiah asked the king if he could
    a. give the Israelites straw to help them
       make better bricks.
    b. start a program called The Great Society
       to help the Jews in exile.
    c. go back and rebuild the city of Jerusalem.
    d. grant the Jews more time off from work.

11. Did the king grant Nehemiah's request?

12. True or False: Nehemiah told the king he
    was sad about Jerusalem.

13. Did you know that travel to Judah would have
    placed Nehemiah in great danger? Nehemiah
    needed letters from the king giving him per-
    mission to pass through enemy territory. The
    king also sent along soldiers to protect
    Nehemiah from harm (Nehemiah 2:7-9).

14. The animal Nehemiah took with him was
    a. his pet goldfish.
    b. his donkey.
    c. a camel with bad breath.
    d. a pet boa constrictor to squeeze his
       opponents to death.

15. True or False: Rebuilding Jerusalem was risky because it was against the emperor's wishes.

16. Who was Nehemiah counting on for his success?

17. Did you know that King David was buried in Jerusalem? (Nehemiah 3:16).

18. The wall was built in a circle, starting and finishing at
    a. Pizza Hut of Jerusalem.
    b. David's tomb.
    c. a statue of Hermes.
    d. the sheep gate.

19. True or False: Everyone was happy to see the new wall being built.

20. True or False: When Nehemiah realized that people were making fun of his efforts to rebuild the wall, he called off the project and went back to Persia.

21. Did you know that half the men had to stand guard, armed with spears, while the other half built the wall? This slowed down their work but protected them against opposition to the project (Nehemiah 4:21).

22. Later, Jerusalem's Jews complained that
    a. they were too poor to feed their families.
    b. they had gotten tired of manna.
    c. there was a shortage of Andy Griffith CDs.
    d. the wall should be painted gold.

23. Nehemiah was angry when he discovered
    a. the leaders had been keeping all the gold paint for themselves.
    b. the paint store wouldn't refund his money.
    c. the rich Jews were taking advantage of their poor relatives.
    d. he wouldn't be paid the thirty silver talents he had been promised.

24. True or False: The leaders promised to return everyone's property and not try to collect any debts.

25. Did you know that when Nehemiah was governor of Judah, he fed a big crowd of more than one hundred people every day? His menu included one beef, six fine sheep, and many chickens (Nehemiah 5:17-18).

26. To show how God would punish any leader who didn't keep his promise to help the poor, Nehemiah
    a. shook his fist.
    b. shook his sash.
    c. invented a dance called the "Hippy Hippy Shake."
    d. told the people how to make milk-shakes.

27. Did the leaders keep their promise to help the poor?

28. True or False: Nehemiah took advantage of all the privileges he was entitled to as governor of Judah.

29. Why didn't Nehemiah claim his big allowance?

30. How many days did it take to build the entire wall?

LAMENTATIONS

1. Where in the Bible can you find the Book of Lamentations?

2. Lamenting means
   a. being sorry about something.
   b. being glad about something.
   c. arguing.
   d. singing.

MUSIC MAN DJ SERVICE

3. Did you know that the prophet Jeremiah wrote Lamentations?

4. In this book, Jeremiah laments
   a. the cancellation of God's promise to provide manna to the people.
   b. the death of Moses.
   c. having to eat spinach lasagna.
   d. the destruction of Jerusalem in 586 BC.

5. Did you know that the Book of Lamentations consists of five poems?

6. True or False: The first poem is about Jerusalem's sorrow.

7. The second poem speaks of God's
   a. love.   c. mercy.
   b. anger.   d. kindness.

8. True or False: Although God punished Jerusalem, he brought the Jews back to himself.

9. True or False: The fifth poem is a prayer for mercy.

10. Think about the last time you asked God for forgiveness. How did you feel? Did you know it is important to ask God for forgiveness when you do wrong?

HOSEA

1. Did you know that the prophet Hosea preached around 721 BC?

2. What was the name of Hosea's wife?

3. God told Hosea to name his son _____ because he would destroy Israel's military power in the valley of _____.

4. Did you know that Hosea's children's names symbolized God's coming punishment for Israel? As you read the Bible, notice how often names were given that had special meanings.

5. Hosea's first daughter was named Lo-Ruhamah, meaning Unloved, because God would no longer show love to the _____.

6. True or False: God told Hosea to name his second son Lo-Ammi, meaning Not My People, because the people of Israel were not His people and He was not their God.

7. Was God planning to be angry with Israel forever?

8. True or False: Gomer was a good wife to Hosea.

9. Hosea planned to
   a. have twelve children with Gomer.
   b. be unfaithful to Gomer for revenge.
   c. win Gomer back.
   d. give Gomer the latest computer for her birthday.

10. How was Gomer's unfaithfulness to Hosea like Israel's unfaithfulness to God?

11. What will happen when Israel returns to God?

12. True or False: God looked kindly upon the Israelite priests during this time.

13. God was upset with the people of Israel for
    a. eating unclean food.
    b. worshipping other gods.
    c. starting a contemporary church service.
    d. playing Christian rock instead of old hymns.

14. God was angry at another country besides Israel. Can you name it?

15. God is angry with the other country for
    a. invading and oppressing Israel.
    b. worshipping false gods.
    c. helping Israel.
    d. eating unclean food.

16. True or False: God says perhaps Israel will look for Him in her suffering.

17. What does God say He wants from His people?

18. The Lord says the people of Israel are like a
   a. wayward servant.
   b. stubborn mule.
   c. bagel with cream cheese.
   d. half-baked loaf of bread.

19. What type of bird does God say the nation of Israel is like?

20. When God compared Israel to this bird, he meant Israel was
   a. strong and true.
   b. soaring upward.
   c. soft and feathery.
   d. flitting from place to place.

21. Did you know that one false god the Israelites worshipped was Baal? Hosea says the Israelites gave Baal corn, wine, oil, and money (Hosea 2:8). The Lord was not pleased when they gave His gifts to a false god.

22. True or False: God said Israel will be punished for her sins.

23. Hosea said that the Israelites would return to Egypt. Why would this be a punishment for them?

24. The false idols the Israelites worshipped were shaped like
    a. Goliath's shield.   c. ravens.
    b. calves.   d. a cedar tree.

25. True or False: Hosea asked the Israelites to return to God.

26. Hosea asked God to
    a. punish the Israelites greatly.
    b. send a plague to the land.
    c. send them into slavery.
    d. forgive their sins.

27. Hosea asked the Israelites to offer God a prayer (Hosea 14:2). Think about your prayers to God. Do you just ask Him to do things for you? Or do you thank Him for all He has done for you?

28. What do the people promise in their prayer?

29. The Lord promised Israel
   a. a new life.
   b. a new health care plan.
   c. that their children will never have to go to school.
   d. that they will never have to eat spinach.

30. Did you know that even though God punished Israel, He loved them all the same? He loves us, too. John 3:16 tells us just how much. Can you say John 3:16 from memory?

JOEL

1. Did you know that the book of Joel makes no mention of any king or foreign nation? This means it is hard for Bible scholars to tell exactly when it was written. However, they believe it was written in the eighth or ninth century, BC.

2. Who wrote the book of Joel?

3. You can find the book of Joel in
   a. the Old Testament, after Hosea.
   b. the New Testament, before Matthew.
   c. the Old Testament, after Daniel.
   d. your Bible's concordance.

4. Joel was a
   a. Levite.
   b. prophet.
   c. tax collector.
   d. Hollywood director.

5. True or False: A prophet tells what God plans to do in the future.

6. Joel talked about a time in the past when the land was filled with
   a. milk and honey.   c. floods.
   b. locusts.   d. thieves.

7. True or False: The people were upset because their crops had been destroyed by bugs.

8. The Lord wanted the people to
   a. invite Him to the Super Bowl.
   b. repent of their sins.
   c. stop eating fruit from the Garden of Eden.
   d. build an ark.

9. True or False: God restored Israel's fertile land.

10. True or False: God told the land and animals not to be afraid.

11. Why should the people be glad?

12. True or False: God will judge the nations in the Land Before Time.

13. Did you know that the term Valley of Jehoshaphat means "Yahweh judges"? Today's English Version of the Bible translates Valley of Jehoshaphat as "Valley of Judgment."

14. Egypt and Edom will be punished for attacking
    a. The United States.
    b. Saudi Arabia.
    c. Jordan.
    d. Judah.

15. Where will the Lord live when he returns to Earth?

MICAH

1. Did you know that the prophet Micah was from Judah? He was afraid his country would be punished by God. He wanted to warn them to repent (Micah 1:9).

2. Who wrote the book of Micah?

3. You can find the book of Micah in
   a. the Old Testament, after the book of Jonah.
   b. the Old Testament, before the book of Genesis.
   c. the New Testament, after Revelation.
   d. the index of the Bible.

4. True or False: Idolatry is the worship of false gods.

5. The country of Judah was guilty of
   a. watching too much TV.
   b. idolatry.
   c. laziness.
   d. being late for school too often.

6. What did Micah say about Samaria?

7. Micah said he would show his sorrow about God's punishment by
   a. writing a Top 40 country western song.
   b. giving more money to the church treasury.
   c. eating locusts and wild honey.
   d. walking naked and howling.

8. True or False: Micah said Judah would not be punished.

9. The people did not like Micah's prophecy (Micah 2:6). Why?

10. Micah said the people wanted a prophet who would
    a. lie.   c. steal.
    b. cheat.   d. sing.

11. True or False: Micah had nothing but good things to say about the rulers of Israel.

12. Did you know that a part of Micah's prophecy is just like Isaiah's? Micah said the mountain where the temple stands will be the highest of all, attracting many people. (Compare Micah 4:1-4 and Isaiah 2:2-4.)

13. True or False: In Micah 4:1-4 and Isaiah 2:2-4 God promises peace. Hint: You may want to read question 12 again while you think about this.

14. Did you know that some prophets took money in exchange for telling people what they wanted to hear instead of the truth? God was very upset with these false prophets (Micah 3:11).

15. The false prophets thought it was all right to lie because
    a. they thought the Lord was with them.
    b. their daughters were beautiful.
    c. they knew they could get away with it.
    d. they were rich.

16. True or False: Micah says that even though Israel will be punished, the country will once again worship the Lord.

17. God promises Israel a ruler out of Bethlehem whose family line can be traced to ancient times. Who do you think this ruler is?

18. True or False: Bethlehem was one of the great cities of Micah's time.

19. The Bible in Today's English Version says:
When he comes, he will rule his people with the strength that comes from the Lord and with the majesty of the Lord God himself. His people will live in safety because people all over the earth will acknowledge his greatness, and he will bring peace (Micah 5:4-5).

In this passage, Micah is talking about Jesus. Think about the power and glory of Jesus.

20. Micah prophesied that Israel would conquer
    a. Assyria.   c. Egypt.
    b. France.   d. the world.

21. True or False: God wants animal sacrifices from Christians.

22. True or False: Evil people who get their treasures dishonestly will enjoy them.

23. Read Micah 18-20. This passage is read in Jewish synagogues on the Day of Atonement.

24. Did you know that the Lord said the evil people of Micah's time followed King Omri's and King Ahab's wicked ways? (Micah 6:16). This means we should follow the Lord's ways over any earthly ruler's.

THE GOSPELS

1. How many Gospels are there in the Bible?

2. In your Bible, you can find the Gospels in
   a. the first part of the New Testament.
   b. the first part of the Old Testament.
   c. the concordance.
   d. the last part of the New Testament.

3. What is a concordance?

4. The Gospels are the books of
   a. Genesis, Exodus, Leviticus, Numbers, and Deuteronomy.
   b. Jude and Revelation.
   c. Matthew, Mark, Luke, and John.
   d. Genesis and Matthew.

5. All four Gospels tell us about
   a. the life and ministry of Jesus.
   b. Paul's life.
   c. the events surrounding Joshua's prophecies.
   d. how to get good grades without doing any work.

6. Your Bible may have red letters in some places. What do they mean?

7. If your Bible has red letters, you can see them in the Gospels and in
   a. Genesis.
   b. the Acts of the Apostles and Revelation.
   c. no other book of the Bible.
   d. Psalms.

8. True or False: Jesus wrote parts of all four Gospels.

9. Did you know that Matthew was also called Levi? (Mark 2:14).

10. Matthew
    a. was the disciple who be-
       trayed Jesus.
    b. collected taxes for
       Rome.
    c. ran the water slide at the
       King's Dominion amuse-
       ment park in Israel.
    d. was a Roman soldier.

11. Matthew traces Jesus' line back
    to King David. Why do you think he stopped
    there?

12. Did you know that the Gospel of Mark is the
    shortest Gospel?

13. True or False: Luke is the longest Gospel.

14. Which Gospel has the most chapters?

15. Did you know that John was one of the dis-
    ciples in Jesus' inner circle?

THE BIRTH OF JESUS

1. True or False: The story of Jesus' birth is found in the book of Matthew.

2. Did you know there were fourteen generations from Abraham to David, fourteen from David to the exile in Babylon, and fourteen from then to Jesus' birth? (Matthew 1:17).

3. When she discovered she would give birth to Jesus, Mary was engaged to
   a. Adam.   c. Moses.
   b. Joseph.   d. Lot.

4. Did you know that Mary's fiancé was a descendant of King David? (Luke 1:27).

5. Who first told Mary she would have a baby?

6. True or False: Mary visited her cousin Elizabeth in Judea after she discovered she would give birth to God's son.

7. True or False: In a dream, an angel told Joseph he should not be afraid to take Mary as his wife.

8. Did you know that Jesus was born in the same town as King David? (Luke 2:4)

9. In which town was Jesus born?

10. Joseph and Mary went to Bethlehem before Jesus was born because
   a. they were on vacation.
   b. a census was being taken.
   c. they won a mini-van in a sweep-stakes and had to go there to claim it.
   d. Joseph had been offered a job as an innkeeper.

11. True or False: King Herod was filled with joy when he was told the news of Jesus' birth.

12. Did you know King Herod told the wise men he wanted to worship Jesus? (Matthew 2:8)

13. The wise men brought Jesus gifts of
    a. gold, frankincense, and myrrh.
    b. pearls, rings, and baby rattles.
    c. diapers, formula, and mohair blankets.
    d. earrings, spices, and a New Testament Bible.

14. True or False: When Mary and Joseph arrived in town, they stayed at the best hotel.

15. The shepherds learned about Jesus' birth from
    a. a talking wolf.
    b. an invitation they received to his baby shower.
    c. angels.
    d. Mary.

16. Did you know Luke traced Jesus' ancestors all the way back to Adam? You can find the record of Jesus' lineage in Luke 3:23-38.

17. True or False: The wise men told King Herod where Jesus was.

18. True or False: Mary selected Jesus' name herself.

19. After Jesus was born, an angel told Joseph in a dream to take his family to
    a. Egypt.   c. China.
    b. Sodom.   d. The North Pole.

20. Joseph, Mary, and Jesus stayed in Egypt until Herod
    a. offered Joseph a job at the palace paying 5,000 talents a year.
    b. repented of his sins.
    c. promised not to kill Jesus.
    d. died.

21. Did you know that Joseph was first told in a dream to go to Israel after Herod's death? In a second dream, he was told to go to Galilee. The family settled there in the town of Nazareth (Matthew 2:22).

22. Jesus was called a _____ because he grew up in Nazareth.

23. Did you know that when Joseph and Mary presented the baby Jesus to the Lord, they sacrificed a pair of doves and two young pigeons? (Luke 2:24).

24. Mary and Joseph offered the sacrifice because
    a. it signified their love for each other.
    b. they could not find a young ram to sacrifice.
    c. it was required by Mosaic Law.
    d. they had no silver for the treasury.

25. What godly man was told he would not die before he saw the Messiah?

26. Jesus was presented to the Lord at the temple in
    a. Nazareth.   c. Bethlehem.
    b. Jerusalem.   d. Egypt.

27. True or False: When the baby Jesus was presented at the temple, two people said that Jesus was the Messiah.

Jesus Grows Up

1. Did you know that Luke is the only Gospel writer who tells us about Jesus' childhood? You can find the story in Luke 2:39-52.

2. True or False: The books of the Bible that tell us about Jesus' life and ministry are called the Gospels.

3. Jesus grew up in the town of
   a. Bethlehem.   c. Paris.
   b. Cairo.   d. Nazareth.

4. Jesus' parents went to Jerusalem every year to celebrate the
   a. birth of Jesus.   c. Passover.
   b. Last Supper.   d. Super Bowl.

5. After their trip to Jerusalem when Jesus was twelve, his parents discovered He was not with their group returning to their home in Nazareth. They went back to Jerusalem to look for Him. How long did it take them to find Him?

6. Joseph and Mary found Jesus
   a. in the Temple, amazing the teachers with his wisdom.
   b. at the home of a relative.
   c. in a small house with a sign that read "Lost and Found."
   d. eating ice cream at a police station.

7. True or False: Jesus was surprised that Mary and Joseph did not know he would be in the temple.

8. One man who was important in Jesus' earthly life was
   a. John the Baptist.
   b. John the Methodist.
   c. John the Presbyterian.
   d. John the Lutheran.

9. Did you know that when John the Baptist was born, his father planned to name him Zechariah? The Holy Spirit led his parents to name him John instead (Luke 1:59-63).

10. John the Baptist ate
    a. granola bars and yogurt.
    b. tree bark and wild honey.
    c. fried bees and chocolate-covered ants.
    d. locusts and wild honey.

11. True or False: John the Baptist preached about Jesus.

12. True or False: John the Baptist said Jesus would baptize with the Holy Spirit.

13. When John the Baptist preached about King Herod, he said that Herod
    a. was a fine king, worthy of worship.
    b. had kept his promise to give every student a computer.
    c. was evil.
    d. had paid John to say good things about him.

14. What happened to John the Baptist after he preached about King Herod Antipas?

15. Who baptized Jesus?

16. After Jesus was baptized, the Holy Spirit came upon him in the form of
    a. a raven.   c. a locust.
    b. an angel.   d. a dove.

17. True or False: Jesus turned stones into bread to show the devil He was God's son.

18. Satan tempted Jesus by asking Him to turn stones into bread because
    a. Satan's bread had burned in the flames of hell.
    b. Jesus' bread would be far better than any bread Satan could make.
    c. Jesus was very hungry and wanted to eat because he had not eaten for forty days.
    d. Satan's bread tasted like brimstone.

19. Did you know that after Jesus was baptized, the Holy Spirit led Jesus to be tempted by Satan? (Matthew 4:1). Although everyone has a chance to do wrong, God gives us the strength to do what is right.

20. Satan told Jesus that if He was the Son of God, He ought to be able to safely jump from the top of the temple and also turn stones into bread. Do you think these were tests of Jesus' pride? Why or why not?

21. True or False: When Satan told Jesus to jump from the top of the temple, Jesus told him that we are not to test God.

22. If Jesus would worship Satan, Satan promised to give Jesus
    a. all the world's kingdoms.
    b. bags of gold.
    c. heaven's gates.
    d. the love of a beautiful woman.

23. Who helped Jesus after he was tempted by Satan?

24. Did you know that Jesus was about thirty years old when He began His ministry? (Luke 3:23).

25. Where did Jesus begin His ministry?

JESUS HEALS THE SICK

1. The Bible tells us about Jesus healing sick people in
   a. the Gospels.
   b. the Old Testament.
   c. Revelation.
   d. the Book of Restoration.

2. Did you know that the first story about Jesus healing someone is in Matthew 8:1-4?

3. True or False: After He healed the sick man, Jesus commanded him to tell everyone that Jesus was the Messiah.

4. Jesus healed the Roman officer's servant by
   a. touching his cloak.
   b. giving him a special medicine.
   c. prescribing aspirin and fruit juice.
   d. giving an order for him to be healed.

5. Did you know that Jesus praised the Roman officer for having great faith? (Matthew 8:10-13).

6. Whose mother-in-law did Jesus heal of a fever?

7. Jesus healed the woman's fever by
   a. touching her forehead.
   b. touching her hand.
   c. giving her two aspirin and advising her to call Him in the morning.
   d. telling her to bury a potato under a maple tree at midnight.

8. Did you know that after Jesus cured the woman's fever, He healed many others to fulfill a prophecy of Isaiah? (Matthew 8:16-17).

9. True or False: When Jesus drove demons from people, the demons proclaimed that Jesus was God's son.

10. True or False: Jesus healed the sick because He wanted everyone to know He was the Messiah.

11. Jesus drove a mob of demons into a
    a. herd of pigs.
    b. school of fish.
    c. horde of evil people.
    d. rock group.

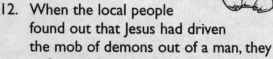

12. When the local people found out that Jesus had driven the mob of demons out of a man, they
    a. feasted for a week.
    b. were afraid.
    c. composed a song in His honor.
    d. made Jesus the town's mayor.

13. True or False: After Jesus drove out the demons, the people asked Him to leave their territory.

14. What did the demon-possessed man want to do after Jesus healed him?

15. True or False: Jesus told the man to go back to his family and to tell everyone what God had done for him.

16. Did the man obey Jesus?

17. To get well from an illness she had suffered from for twelve years, a woman touched Jesus'
    a. cloak.   c. feet.
    b. cup.   d. hand.

18. Jesus said the woman had been cured by her
    a. money.   c. courage.
    b. beauty.   d. faith.

19. Did you know that when the woman was healed, Jesus was on his way to an official's house to heal a little girl?

20. True or False: When Jesus arrived at the official's house, the little girl had already died.

21. Jesus said that the child was not dead, but only _____.

22. Right after Jesus brought the little girl back to life, He healed
    a. a little boy who had only two fish and a loaf of bread for lunch.
    b. two blind men.
    c. three blind mice.
    d. ten lepers.

23. What did Jesus tell the people He healed?

24. Did the people obey Jesus?

25. Did you know that after Jesus healed a man who could not speak, the Pharisees said Jesus' power came from the leader of demons? (Matthew 9:34). This is a very evil thing to say, because Jesus' power comes from God.

LUKE TELLS US ABOUT JESUS

1. Where is Luke's Gospel located in the Bible?

2. Did you know that Luke wrote the Acts of the Apostles?

3. Where can you find the Acts of the Apostles in the Bible?

4. True or False: Luke is the only Gospel writer to tell us anything about Jesus' boyhood.

5. Can you name all four Gospels?

6. True or False: Jesus healed many people during His ministry on Earth.

7. Some important people were mad at Jesus because He ate with
   a. tax collectors and outcasts.
   b. no one—He ate alone.
   c. His family instead of them.
   d. His favorite disciples.

8. True or False: Jesus showed us it is all right to prepare food on the Sabbath.

9. To show it is all right to take care of sick people on the Sabbath, Jesus healed
   a. a man with a soccer injury.
   b. schoolchildren of chicken pox.
   c. a man with a paralyzed hand.
   d. a computer with a virus.

10. True or False: When His enemies saw Jesus healing on the Sabbath, they were happy.

11. A disciple is a
    a. follower.
    b. teacher of false doctrine.
    c. wife of an epistle.
    d. person in charge of computer disks.

12. Jesus chose twelve disciples. How many of them can you name?

13. Which famous sermon did Jesus preach soon after he chose his disciples?

14. True or False: Jesus said we should hate our enemies.

15. Think about a time when someone was mean to you. How did you feel? Was it easy to love and forgive that person?

16. The King James Version of the Bible quotes Jesus as saying, "And as ye would that men should do to you, do ye also to them" (Luke 6:31). This is called the Golden Rule. What is the meaning of the Golden Rule?

17. True or False: When you see someone who is wrong, you should tell that person right away without worrying about your own faults.

18. While Jesus was visiting Simon the Pharisee, a sinful woman
    a. washed His feet with her tears.
    b. tempted Him.
    c. danced for Him.
    d. peeled grapes and fed them to Him.

19. When Simon the Pharisee saw the woman, he
    a. clapped for her.
    b. invited her to eat with them.
    c. asked her to marry him.
    d. said that Jesus shouldn't let a sinful woman touch Him.

20. True or False: Although the woman was sinful, she was trying to show Jesus how much she loved Him.

21. What did Jesus say to the woman after her visit?

22. True or False: Jesus had no followers who were women.

LUKE TELLS US
WHAT JESUS SAID

1. What is a parable?

2. Jesus told many lessons in parables because
   a. he enjoyed confusing everyone just for sport.
   b. he knew just how to spin a yarn.
   c. everyone understood right away.
   d. his disciples could understand them, but not everyone else.

3. True or False: Jesus revered his mother, Mary, over everyone else.

4. When Jesus performed miracles, some people thought he was the resurrected
   a. John the Baptist.   c. Paul.
   b. Moses.   d. Lot.

5. What does the word resurrected mean?

6. True or False: Jesus predicted His own death and resurrection.

7. Jesus said that, to follow Him, you must forget yourself and put Him first (Luke 9:23). How do you do this in your own life?

8. Did you know that once when Jesus was praying, his face glowed and his clothes became dazzling white? This is called the transfiguration (Luke 9:29).

9. During the transfiguration, Jesus was visited by
   a. Noah.
   b. the three wise men.
   c. John the Baptist.
   d. Moses and Elijah.

10. What did Jesus' visitors talk to Him about?

11. Did you know that after Jesus was visited during the transfiguration, God's voice came from a cloud. God said, "This is my beloved son; hear Him" (Luke 9:35).

12. The disciples who saw the transfiguration and heard God's voice
    a. rejoiced and told everyone right away.
    b. were afraid and told no one.
    c. telephoned Eyewitness News.
    d. posted pictures and RealAudio on the Internet.

13. True or False: Jesus' disciples wondered who would be the most important among themselves in heaven.

14. Who did Jesus say would be the most important disciple in heaven?

15. When a person who was not a disciple cast out demons in Jesus' name, the disciples
    a. told him to stop.
    b. rejoiced.
    c. told him to be wary of demons.
    d. tried to take credit.

16. What did Jesus tell the disciples about the man casting out demons?

17. Did you know it was God's plan for Jesus' death on the cross to take place in Jerusalem? Moses and Elijah talked to him about it during the transfiguration (Luke 9:30-31). Jesus set out for Jerusalem with God's plan in mind (Luke 9:51).

18. True or False: When a village in Samaria refused to receive Jesus, the disciples pleaded with Jesus to forgive the people of the village.

19. Concerning this village, Jesus told the disciples
   a. to set it on fire.
   b. to rename it "Petra" after Peter.
   c. not to be unforgiving toward the citizens of the town.
   d. He would eat the Last Supper in this town.

20. True or False: After Jesus spoke to the people in the village, they decided to let him pass through.

21. Did you know that Jesus chose another seventy men to go before him into each town he would be visiting? (Luke 10:1, King James Version). Some Bibles give the number as seventy-two (Today's English Version).

22. When visiting the towns, Jesus told the seventy workers to take
    a. plenty of money.
    b. their credit cards.
    c. an angel on each shoulder.
    d. nothing.

23. How would the workers be taken care of?

24. Jesus told the workers he was sending them out as
    a. lambs among wolves.
    b. doves among hawks.
    c. sheep among lions.
    d. fish among sharks.

25. True or False: When the seventy returned to Jesus, they told him they were amazed by the power Jesus had given them.

THE PRODIGAL SON

1. Who told the story of the prodigal son?

2. Where can you find the story of the prodigal son?

3. True or False: Like many of Jesus' stories, the parable of the prodigal son appears more than once in the Bible.

4. What does the word "prodigal" mean?

5. In the story, how many sons did the wealthy man have?

6. The younger son asked his father to
   a. give him his share of his inheritance.
   b. let him marry the richest girl in town.
   c. allow him to go to the skating rink with the church youth group.
   d. loan him some money to go to the mall.

7. An "inheritance" is
   a. a hair transplant.
   b. property that is passed on when some-one dies.
   c. nose hair.
   d. Hebrew for "cash."

8. True or False: The father did as the younger son asked.

9. The younger son
   a. invested the money in comic books.
   b. bought Mark McGwire's seventieth home run baseball.
   c. wasted his money.
   d. buried the money in the back yard.

10. After the son's money was gone, he got a job
    a. at a fast food restaurant.
    b. herding sheep.
    c. as a used car salesman.
    d. tending pigs.

97

11. Did you know that the younger son was about to starve from hunger before he finally decided to go back to his father and ask forgiveness? (Luke 15:17). The son's desperate state is much like the sad situation many sinners will come to before they repent and ask God for forgiveness.

12. True or False: When the father saw the son returning, he was angry and told him to go back to tending pigs.

13. When the son returned, the father gave him
    a. a whipping.
    b. a video game play station.
    c. a job.
    d. a ring, a robe, and shoes.

14. True or False: The father threw a big party to celebrate.

15. True or False: The father was so happy to have the younger brother home, he forgot all about the older brother.

16. When the older son heard about the welcome home party, he
    a. hired a band to play at the party.
    b. hugged and kissed his brother.
    c. gave his brother the keys to his car.
    d. was angry.

17. Why did the older brother feel this way?

18. The father said to the older brother,
    a. "Leave my house."
    b. "I always liked your younger brother better than you."
    c. "Everything I have is yours and we are close."
    d. "You always were a tattletale."

19. True or False: The father convinced the older brother to celebrate his brother's homecoming.

THE GOOD SAMARITAN

1. Where can you find the story of the Good Samaritan?

2. True or False: The parable of the Good Samaritan can be found in all four Gospels.

3. Did you know that the Gospel of John does not record any of Jesus' parables?

4. A parable is
   a. a biography.
   b. a pair of pears.
   c. a story that teaches a lesson.
   d. a fable told by Aesop.

5. Jesus told the story of the Good Samaritan to answer the question,
   a. "Can I follow you?"
   b. "What can I eat?"
   c. "Is it OK for me to watch PG-13 movies?"
   d. "Who is my neighbor?"

6. Jesus was asked this question by
   a. a lawyer.
   b. an evil woman.
   c. Satan.
   d. one of the Seven Dwarves.

7. In the story, a man needed help because he
   a. had eaten too much and needed to be carried.
   b. didn't know who his neighbor was.
   c. had been beaten and robbed.
   d. refused to ask for directions even though he had been driving for hours.

8. True or False: When the priest and Levite saw the man lying on the side of the road, they stopped and helped him.

9. To what city was the man going when he was beaten and robbed? Hint: The Jews had taken it by knocking down its walls with the sound of trumpets and a shout.

10. Who stopped to help the injured man?

11. Did you know that the road to Jericho was very dangerous? Thieves and bandits could hide in its mountainous terrain, waiting to rob travelers. This is probably why it is the setting for the parable of the Good Samaritan.

12. Did you know that the Samaritan was an unlikely person to help a Jew? Jews were their hated enemies. This is demonstrated by the Samaritan village that refused to offer Jesus a place to stay when they discovered He was on His way to Jerusalem. Read Luke 9:51-56 to learn more.

13. The salves the Samaritan applied to the man's wounds were
    a. Solarcaine spray and Bactine.
    b. Dr. Feelgood's Miracle Salve and Potion.
    c. oil and wine.
    d. rubbing alcohol and butter.

14. True or False: The Samaritan stayed with the man the following day.

15. The Samaritan took the man to
    a. dinner at Burger King.
    b. a dark alley and robbed him.
    c. an inn.
    d. a revival meeting at church.

16. How much did the Samaritan give the inn-keeper to care for the man until he was well?

17. Did you know that two denarii was equal to two days' pay?

18. True or False: Jesus asked the lawyer to iden-tify which person was the man's neighbor.

19. Who do you think was the neighbor to the man: the Levite, the priest, or the Samaritan?

20. Jesus told the lawyer,
    a. "You are like the Levite."
    b. "Only good people are your neighbors."
    c. "You need to be concerned only about people who go to your school."
    d. "Go and do likewise."

JESUS' RESURRECTION

1. True or False: You can read about Jesus' resurrection in all four Gospels.

2. Who were the three women who went to Jesus' grave the day he arose?

3. When the women saw the grave, they discovered that the covering of the grave had been rolled back by
   a. an angel of the Lord.   c. Jesus.
   b. Goliath.   d. Samson.

4. The one who rolled the stone back told the women,
   a. "You will be punished for stealing the body."
   b. "Expect an earthquake."
   c. "Fear not, for Jesus has risen."
   d. "I'm tired from all that work and I want something to eat."

5. True or False: Jesus' disciples believed the women when they told them that Jesus had risen from the dead.

6. Who went to the grave to see if what the women said was true?

7. True or False: Jesus appeared to Mary Magdalene after He arose.

8. When Jesus saw His disciples after He had risen, He said,
   a. "See, I told you so!"
   b. "Is there any bread left over from the Last Supper?"
   c. "Peace be unto you."
   d. "I really missed you these past three days."

9. He said this because He
   a. wanted to show He was right.
   b. was hungry.
   c. wanted to reassure them.
   d. was glad to be back.

THE LORD'S PRAYER

1. Did you know you can find The Lord's Prayer in two places in the Bible? You can read it in Matthew 6:9-13 and Luke 11:2-3.

2. Can you recite The Lord's Prayer by heart?

3. Jesus taught the disciples this prayer because

   a. one of them had asked Him to teach them how to pray.
   b. He was angered by their awkward prayers.
   c. otherwise, they would sing psalms off-key.
   d. they needed a new version for Dial-a-Prayer.

4. According to The Lord's Prayer, where is God the Father?

5. What does Jesus mean when He says God's name should be hallowed?

6. What do you do to honor God's name?

7. True or False: Obeying God's commandment not to take His name in vain is one way to keep God's name hallowed.

8. True or False: In Matthew's Gospel, Jesus told them how to pray because He was angered by the hypocrites' loud praying.

9. What is a hypocrite?

10. Did you know that there is no contradiction between the two accounts of Jesus' sharing the prayer? The Lord's Prayer was apparently taught at two different times.

11. True or False: Once you learn The Lord's Prayer, there is no need to pray on your own.

12. The Lord's Prayer says to ask God for enough food every day. Can you remember the last time you were really hungry? Does remembering this make you think about how important it is to ask God to take care of you?

13. Why is this prayer called The Lord's Prayer?

14. When Jesus says we should ask God to forgive us as we forgive others, it means
    a. God should forgive us whether we forgive others or not.
    b. we should not owe anyone any money.
    c. we should not loan anyone any money.
    d. God will forgive us when we forgive others.

15. True or False: You are supposed to pray The Lord's Prayer every day on the radio to show how wonderful you are.

Paul Speaks About Love

1. Who wrote 1 Corinthians?

2. The Corinthians who received the letter were
   a. members of the Corinthian Country Club.
   b. members of the church at Corinth.
   c. makers of Corinthian leather.
   d. reporters for the *Corinthian Courant.*

3. Did you know that in some older versions of the Bible, the word "charity" is used in place of the word "love" in Paul's first letter to the Corinthians. If you have ever heard someone speak of showing another person Christian charity, it means showing kindness and compassion.

4. True or False: Fine preaching makes up for a lack of love.

5. You don't need love if you have
   a. lots of money.
   b. faith.
   c. plenty of lambs to sacrifice.
   d. none of the above. You must have love.

6. When Paul says love is not puffed
   up, he means love is not
   a. fat.
   b. filled with air.
   c. inflated like a
      blowfish.
   d. proud.

7. What does Paul mean when he says that love
   is not provoked? (1 Corinthians 13:5)

8. True or False: We know everything there is
   to know while we live on earth.

9. Of faith, hope, and love, which is the
   greatest?

10. Why do you think love is so important?

THE FRUIT OF THE SPIRIT

1. The fruit of the Spirit is
   a. an orange.
   b. a lemon.
   c. a set of attitudes you'll have if you love God.
   d. the title of a Dr. Seuss book.

2. Where in the Bible can we can learn about the fruit of the Spirit?

3. Who told us about the fruit of the Spirit?

4. The Galatians were
   a. members of a group of churches in Galatia.
   b. a galaxy of stars.
   c. bugs from a popular video game.
   d. aliens from another galaxy.

5. Did you know that you can not find Galatia on a modern day map? Galatia was the name of a region in Asia Minor—modern day Turkey.

6. One fruit of the Spirit is "love." Can you name at least one other letter where Paul writes about love?

7. When Paul speaks of joy, he means
   a. a dishwashing detergent.
   b. happiness in the Lord.
   c. a baby kangaroo.
   d. Joseph's nickname.

8. Did you know there is more than one type of peace? You can be at peace with yourself, which means you like yourself. You can be at peace with others, which means you aren't fighting with anyone. On a national level, this means the country is not at war with another country. Most importantly, you can be at peace with the Lord. This does not mean you are perfect. When you are saved, you know the Lord has forgiven your sins. This puts you at peace with Him.

9. You are long-suffering when
   a. you can sit through math class without passing a note.
   b. you don't fall asleep when the teacher is talking about history.
   c. you can forgive other people when they sin against you.
   d. you will eat vegetables three meals in a row.

10. Paul names "gentleness" as a fruit of the Spirit (Galatians 5:22). Who is the most gentle person you know? What is he or she like?

11. True or False: "Goodness" is a fruit of the Spirit.

12. True or False: A person of faith must see something to believe it.

13. "Meekness" means a person is
   a. a wimp.   c. strong, but kind to others.
   b. quiet.   d. mousy.

14. The King James Version says that "temperance" is a fruit of the Spirit. Temperance is
    a. another word for heating and cooling your house.
    b. running a fever.
    c. not going outside when it is too hot or too cold.
    d. controlling your self and not going to the extreme.

15. True or False: Paul wrote about the fruit of the Spirit because he wanted everybody to live by the letter of the Mosaic law.

16. Paul says that those living with the fruit of the Spirit have crucified the flesh. This means they
    a. have Christian tattoos.
    b. have pierced their ears.
    c. have skin as wrinkled as a prune.
    d. don't think about their bodies as much as they think about living for Christ.

17. When we walk in the Spirit, it means that
    a. we obey Christ.
    b. a cloud surrounds us.
    c. we play basketball in high-heeled Easy Spirit pumps.
    d. Mom won't drive us to soccer practice.

18. True or False: It is all right to be jealous of other people.

19. Why is it important to obey Christ?

20. Now that you have learned about the fruit of the Spirit, can you name all nine?

1 PETER

1. 1 Peter is a letter written by
   a. Peter.
   b. Paul.
   c. Mary.
   d. Moses.

2. True or False: The author of 1 Peter was one of Jesus' apostles.

3. Some scholars think that Peter was the leader of the apostles because he
   a. liked to write letters.
   b. is named first in every list of the apostles in the Bible.
   c. had the most money.
   d. was the only one with Internet access.

4. Peter wrote this letter to
   a. Jesus.
   b. persecuted Christians.
   c. rich Christians.
   d. a woman who wanted to publish his life story.

5. In 1 Peter 1:4, Peter speaks of an inheritance, meaning that the people he writes to will have
   a. their fortunes told.
   b. more money in the future.
   c. personal hair-dressers.
   d. eternal life.

STYLING SEMINAR
✓ Volumizing
✓ Hair Sculpting

6. True or False: Peter says that when we live like Jesus, we will not live like the rest of the world lives.

7. What does the word "redeemed" mean?

8. Peter says we were redeemed by
   a. Jesus.
   b. silver.
   c. a cents-off coupon.
   d. the good things we do for others.

9. Peter says that Christians should not envy other people (1 Peter 2:1). Which of God's Ten Commandments means the same thing?

10. We should also put aside evil speaking. What commandment does this remind you of?

11. Peter says that Christians should be like
    a. newborn babes.
    b. goats.
    c. sheep without a shepherd.
    d. Superman.

12. The milk of the word will
    a. taste sour.
    b. turn to yogurt.
    c. spill on your books.
    d. make Christians grow.

13. Peter says that Christians are like
    a. pet rocks.
    b. red bricks.
    c. living stones.
    d. wood.

14. True or False: Christians are building a spiritual house.

15. Did you know that the name Peter means "rock"?

16. True or False: Jesus is the chief cornerstone.

17. What does Peter mean when he says that Jesus is the stone of stumbling and rock of offense?

18. True or False: It is important for Christians to live as Christ wants because the world is watching us.

19. Peter calls Christians "sojourners." What is a sojourner?

20. True or False: When Peter compares Christians to pilgrims, he is talking about the people who sailed to America on the *Mayflower*.

21. Christians should
    a. disobey all laws made by men.
    b. obey the laws of their nations.
    c. fight against the law.
    d. obey the laws they think are right.

22. True or False: It is all right to be mean to someone who is mean to you first.

23. When people say mean things to us, we should
    a. remember how Jesus trusted God.
    b. gossip about them.
    c. take them to court and let the judge decide what to do.
    d. tell the teacher.

24. Peter compares the Christians to
    a. blocks of granite.   c. lost sheep.
    b. diamonds.   d. all of the above.

25. Jesus spoke about lost sinners in three parables. Do you remember what they are?

26. Peter refers to Jesus as a shepherd. What famous psalm also says he is a shepherd?

27. What does the word "submit" mean?

28. True or False: Peter says that wives should only submit to their husbands if the husbands follow Christ.

29. Did you know that Peter offers hope to the wives of unsaved men? He tells them to obey God and to show their husbands how to live like Christians. Their lives may inspire their husbands to turn to Christ.

30. True or False: Christian women should depend completely on lipstick, perfume, and jewels to make them pretty.

31. Peter tells husbands to
   a. give their wives anything they want.
   b. take their wives out to dinner three times a week.
   c. give their wives a dozen roses for every wedding anniversary.
   d. honor their wives.

32. When Peter says that the wife is the weaker vessel, he means that the wife is
    a. not as strong physically as her husband.
    b. dumb.
    c. like a tiny blood vessel.
    d. like a rowboat.

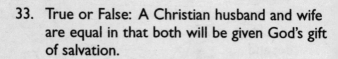

33. True or False: A Christian husband and wife are equal in that both will be given God's gift of salvation.

34. True or False: Those who suffer because they are Christians are blessed.

35. Peter says that Christians should answer questions about the Christian faith with
    a. anger.   c. a funny greeting card.
    b. meekness.   d. an e-mail message.

36. Jesus spoke about suffering and meekness in a famous sermon. Do you remember the name of the sermon?

37. Did you know that when Peter says, "Love will cover a multitude of sins," this is a quote from Proverbs 10:12?

38. When Peter says that love will cover a multitude of sins, he means that
    a. sleeping sins will stay warm.
    b. a sinner can take refuge in a bomb shelter.
    c. love has its limits.
    d. when you love people, you can forget about their sins.

39. True or False: Peter says that Christians should rejoice at being tried, because they share in suffering with Christ.

40. In 1 Peter 4:15, Peter cautions Christians not to
    a. be busybodies.
    b. be busy building up their bodies.
    c. busy themselves listening to hard rock music.
    d. watch PG rated movies.

41. Who are our earthly shepherds in the church today?

42. Young people should submit to their
    a. impulse to play computer games all day.
    b. elders.
    c. sisters.
    d. friends at school.

43. The Ten Commandments say, "Honor thy father and thy mother" (Exodus 20:12). How is this commandment like Peter's advice to young people?

44. Who is the enemy of Christians?

45. What is the last word in Peter's first letter?

2 PETER

1. How do we know that Peter is the author of 2 Peter?

2. Did you know that 2 Peter was written in AD 66, one year after 1 Peter was written?

3. Peter wrote his second letter to
   a. Christians in Asia Minor.
   b. Christians in the United States.
   c. Jews in Israel.
   d. Mrs. Witherspoon's fifth grade class.

4. Why is it important for us to study Peter's letters?

5. True or False: Peter says we are more like Jesus when we give up worldly things.

6. Peter lists eight traits that a Christian should have. One of these is faith. Can you name the others?

7. Did you know that Peter was probably over seventy years old and in a Roman prison when he wrote this letter?

8. When Peter says "shortly I must put off this my tabernacle," he means that he will soon
   a. stop going to church.
   b. take his name out of the running for church deacon.
   c. die.
   d. join another church.

9. True or False: Peter was an eyewitness to God's confirmation that Jesus is the Messiah.

10. True or False: God will spare false prophets.

11. False prophets
    a. lie.
    b. disrespect God.
    c. tell people what they want to hear.
    d. all of the above.

12. An Old Testament false prophet, Balaam, the
    son of Beor, was rebuked by
    a. a talking donkey.
    b. the Apostle Peter.
    c. a talking pig.
    d. Joseph of Arimathea.

13. What does Peter mean when he says "a pig
    that has been washed goes back to roll in the
    mud"? (2 Peter 2:22, Today's English Version)

14. The Day of the Lord will arrive
    a. as fast as a Domino's Pizza delivery guy.
    b. as a thief in the night.
    c. as soon as the circus comes to town.
    d. absolutely, positively, on July 7, 2077.

15. True or False: Peter warns Christians not to
    fall away from the faith.

Answer Key

The Cruise of a Lifetime

1. a. Genesis. The story is told in chapters 6-9.

2. False. God was angry that the people were so evil (Genesis 6:5-6).

3. b. destroy all the people, animals, and birds He had created (Genesis 6:7).

4. True (Genesis 6:9-10).

5. Noah had three sons (Genesis 6:9).

6. Noah's three sons were named Shem, Ham, and Japheth (Genesis 6:9).

8. A ritually clean beast is acceptable to God for sacrifice. A ritually unclean beast is not. Although God asked for animal sacrifices under Old Testament law, Christians do not make animal sacrifices. Instead, we give money to the work of the church. It is also important to give

our time to the church. We can do that by helping with Vacation Bible School, babysitting in the nursery, or in other ways. How can you help your Sunday School teacher or other adults in church?

9. c. 600 years old (Genesis 7:6).

10. It rained forty days and forty nights (Genesis 7:12).

12. a. 7-1/2 months. The flood began on the seventeenth day of the second month (Genesis 7:11). And Noah was able to see the tops of the mountains again on the first day of the tenth month (Genesis 8:5).

14. False. The first bird Noah sent out from the ark was a raven (Genesis 8:7).

15. d. an olive branch (Genesis 8:11). This showed Noah that the water had started to go down.

16. True (Genesis 8:13).

17. c. built an altar to God and made sacrifices upon it (Genesis 8:20).

18. True (Genesis 8:21 and 9:11).

19. God was pleased with the smell of the sacrifices Noah made after the flood. The pleasant odor caused Him to promise not to destroy the earth by flood again (Genesis 8:20-22).

20. A rainbow reminds us of God's promise (Genesis 9:13).

A TOWERING PROBLEM

1. The story of the Tower of Babel can be found in Genesis 11:1-9.

2. True (Genesis 11:1).

3. d. an unspecified language. Everyone spoke the same language (Genesis 11:1), but the Bible does not say what language the people spoke.

5. c. brick (Genesis 11:3).

6. True (Genesis 11:4-5).

7. d. reach to heaven (Genesis 11:6).

8. False (Genesis 11:6-7).

9. d. made the people all speak different languages so
    they couldn't finish the work (Genesis 11:7).

10. The story of the Tower of Babel is important because:
    1. It shows us that God places limits upon mankind
        (Genesis 11:6).
    2. It explains why we speak different languages
        (Genesis 11:6-9).
    3. It shows how God scattered the people all over
        the face of the earth (Genesis 11:9).

GOD'S PROMISE TO ABRAHAM

2. You can find the story of God's promise to Abraham
    in Genesis 16-19.

3. True (Genesis 17:4-5).

4. Abraham was ninety-nine years old when God
    appeared to him (Genesis 17:1).

5. c. obey Him (Genesis 17:1).

6. b. bowed down, touching his face to the ground (Genesis 17:3).

7. A covenant is a solemn promise. For example, when we are baptized, we promise God we will follow Him.

8. True (Genesis 17:2).

9. a. a member of a future generation.

10. d. the land of Canaan (Genesis 17:8). Abraham was living in Canaan as a foreigner at that time.

11. True. The covenant applied to Abraham and to future generations as well (Genesis 17:8).

12. c. Abraham was to be the father of many nations (Genesis 17:5).

13. True (Genesis 17:6).

14. True (Genesis 17:7).

15. Abraham's wife was named Sarai before God renamed her Sarah (Genesis 17:15).

16. c. have a baby (Genesis 17:16).

17. b. laughed (Genesis 17:17). Abraham did not think it was possible for him and his wife to be new parents because they were old.

18. God promised a baby boy (Genesis 17:16).

19. c. was ninety years old, which is usually too old to have a baby (Genesis 17:17).

20. Abraham was ninety-nine years old when God promised him a baby (Genesis 17:17).

22. c. a person who receives an inheritance. In biblical times, the firstborn son usually was next in line for his father's position and money when the father died. This meant that after the father died, the oldest son became head of the family.

23. False (Genesis 17:19).

24. True (Genesis 17:13).

25. Like Abraham, Christians are people of God. We are Abraham's descendants.

THE TEN COMMANDMENTS

2. False: Exodus and Deuteronomy are both Old Testament books. Exodus is the second book of the Bible and Deuteronomy is the fifth book.

3. Moses wrote the first five books of the Bible.

5. The five books of the Pentateuch are Genesis, Exodus, Leviticus, Numbers, and Deuteronomy.

6. b. Mount Sinai (Exodus 19:20).

8. b. God had brought them out of slavery in Egypt. You can read about this event in Exodus 5:1-15:21.

9. True (Exodus 20:3; Deuteronomy 5:7).

10. The First Commandment is the most important because it defines our relationship to God. God wants us to love Him, just as He loves us. If we do not love God, we can not keep the other commandments.

11. False. The Second Commandment tells us not to make any idols (Exodus 20:4; Deuteronomy 5:8-9).

12. God means we are not to call His name unless we are praying to Him or worshipping Him. Think about how you would feel if people kept saying your name, attracting your attention for no reason. Would you feel angry? Would you be upset? God does not want us to call His name unless we mean to speak to Him or to praise His name.

13. d. keep holy, cease work, and remember His people's deliverance from Egypt (Exodus 20:8-11; Deuteronomy 5:12-15).

14. False (Exodus 20:8-11; Deuteronomy 5:12-15). However, Jesus said that necessary work may be done on the Sabbath (Matthew 12:1-8; Mark 2:23-27; Luke 6:1-5).

15. God wants us to rest every seventh day because He rested on the seventh day after He created the world (Exodus 20:11). By resting on the seventh day, we are honoring God by being like Him in this way.

17. We attend church on Sunday, read the Bible, rest, and otherwise follow God's instructions.

18. c. father and mother (Exodus 20:12; Deuteronomy 5:16). Our parents have an important place in our lives because God has entrusted them to care for us on earth. God wants us to give them special respect and honor. However, we should also treat our teachers, pastor, and friends with respect.

19. True (Exodus 20:13; Deuteronomy 5:17). Life belongs to God the Creator, not to us.

20. We can find out how God established marriage in Genesis 2:21-34.

21. c. steal (Exodus 20:15; Deuteronomy 5:19). Showing love for others includes respecting the things they own. That is why we should not rob people.

22. We should not lie, but tell the truth. Giving false information is a sin against the person we're lying to. Lies hurt other people. A liar is not showing love to God or to other people.

24. d. wish we had our neighbor's stuff. Do you know someone who would like something you have, such as a movie video or a computer game? Why not share it with that person? You may make a new friend.

25. a. Leviticus.

27. b. stone tablets (Deuteronomy 5:22).

28. False. While Moses was with God on the mountain for forty days, the people made a false idol. Moses was so angry with their disobedience to God, he broke the tablets when he came down the mountain (Deuteronomy 9:17).

29. These are the Ten Commandments:
    1. Worship no god but God.
    2. Do not worship idols.
    3. Do not take the Lord's name in vain.
    4. Remember the Sabbath day and keep it holy.
    5. Honor your mother and father.
    6. Do not murder.
    7. Do not commit adultery.
    8. Do not steal.
    9. Do not lie.
    10. Do not covet.

Joshua's Famous Battle

2. True (Numbers 27:18-23).

4. c. the death of Moses.

5. The book of Joshua is found in the Old Testament.

6. As its title suggests, Joshua wrote the book of Joshua.

7. c. Jordan River (Joshua 1:2).

8. True (Joshua 1:9).

9. c. the home of a wicked woman (Joshua 2:1).

10. True (Joshua 2:2-7).

12. a. on the roof (Joshua 2:6).

14. True (Joshua 2:10-14).

15. Rahab protected the spies because she knew they were there to claim the land for the Lord's people (Joshua 2:9).

17. The ark of the covenant was a wooden box covered with gold and built to God's specification. It contained the stone tablets on which the Ten Commandments were written.

18. A total of forty thousand men crossed the plains of Jericho, ready to fight for the Lord (Joshua 4:13).

19. b. eaten food grown in the promised land (Joshua 5:11).

20. Manna was the food God rained down upon the Israelites to provide food for them while they were wandering in the wilderness on their way to the promised land. God rained fresh manna for them every day (Exodus 16:14-18).

22. False. The walls came tumbling down by the sounds of horns and a shout. The priests blew horns for seven days as they walked around the city with the ark of the covenant (Joshua 6:3-16).

23. The lives of Rahab and her household were spared during the fall of Jericho. This is important because it shows God always keeps his promises (Joshua 6:17 and 22-23).

24. b. put into the Lord's treasury (Joshua 6:19).

25. True (Joshua 6:27).

David Fights Goliath

1. a. 1 Samuel. Look in Chapter 17, verses 1-54.

3. False. Goliath wore bronze armor all over his body. A
        soldier went before him to carry his shield.
        Goliath carried a large spear (1 Samuel 17:5-7).

4. False. They were too scared to fight Goliath
        (1 Samuel 17:11).

5. David was taking food to his three older brothers
    who were soldiers in battle (1 Samuel 17:17).

6. b. tended sheep (1 Samuel 17:15).

7. Gath was located in Philistia.

8. True (1 Samuel 17:23).

10. False. Eliab, the oldest, scolded David and asked him who was tending his sheep (1 Samuel 17:28).

11. a. wondered how Goliath dared to defy the army of the living God (1 Samuel 17:26).

12. c. was only a boy (1 Samuel 17:33).

14. True (1 Samuel 17:36).

15. c. he couldn't walk in it because he wasn't used to such cumbersome armor (1 Samuel 17:39).

16. David picked up five stones (1 Samuel 17:40).

17. False. Goliath made fun of David (1 Samuel 17:43-44).

18. d. There is a God in Israel (1 Samuel 17:46).

19. True. The stone hit his forehead and Goliath fell face down to the ground (1 Samuel 17:49).

20. a. chased the Philistines back to their own country (1 Samuel 17:52).

Elisha Performs Many Miracles

1. False (1 Kings 19:19).

2. b. 2 Kings.

4. Enoch was taken to heaven without dying because he walked with the Lord (Genesis 5:23-24).

5. True (2 Kings 2:9).

6. b. dividing the Jordan River and walking on dry land (2 Kings 2:14). He struck the water with Elijah's cloak, and the water parted.

7. True (2 Kings 2:15). This is important because their recognition of him helped to establish Elisha as a prophet.

8. c. made the water pure (2 Kings 2:20-22).

9. c. bald (2 Kings 2:23).

11. c. rebelled against Israel (2 Kings 3:5).

12. True (2 Kings 3:16).

13. c. they thought the water they saw around the camp was blood (2 Kings 3:21-23). When the Moabites saw water on what had been dry land, they thought it was blood because the sunlight hit it in such a way that the water appeared to be red. They thought the three armies had killed each other, so they decided to rob the camp.

14. They were attacked by the Israelites (2 Kings 3:24).

15. True (2 Kings 3:24-25).

16. a. was in debt (2 Kings 4:1).

17. d. a small jar of olive oil (2 Kings 4:2). Elisha told her to get jars from her neighbors and pour the oil into them (2 Kings 4:3).

18. The woman poured the small amount of olive oil she had in her house into all the jars. When they were all filled, the oil stopped.

19. True (2 Kings 4:7). She sold the oil for money.

20. No, she did not accept his offer (2 Kings 4:13).

21. b. promising her that she would have a baby (2 Kings 4:17). The woman was rich, but she had no son. She gave birth to a baby boy as Elisha had promised.

22. c. setting up a room for him to stay in when he visited (2 Kings 4:10).

23. True (2 Kings 4:18-37).

24. a. brought the boy back from the dead (2 Kings 4:18-37).

26. This miracle might make you think of Jesus feeding five thousand men, plus untold women and children, with the contents of a small boy's lunch. Read about it in Matthew 14:13-21, Mark 6:30-44, Luke 9:10-17, and John 6:1-14.

27. True (2 Kings 4:38-41). There had been a famine, so food was scarce. The cook used poisonous gourds by mistake. Elisha made the stew pure so they could eat it.

28. False (2 Kings 5:1). Naaman was a respected *Syrian* commander.

29. a. leprosy (2 Kings 5:1).

30. A servant girl suggested that Elisha could cure Naaman (2 Kings 5:2-3).

32. c. "I do not have the power of God! The Syrian king wants to quarrel with me" (2 Kings 5:7).

33. True (2 Kings 5:8).

34. a. wash seven times in the Jordan River (2 Kings 5:10).

35. b. was angry (2 Kings 5:11). He did not understand why he could not wash himself in a river in Damascus and become cured there.

36. False. Naaman was cured as soon as he rose from bathing in the Jordan River the seventh time (2 Kings 5:14).

37. Naaman vowed to worship Elisha's God (2 Kings 5:18).

39. d. two mule loads (2 Kings 5:17).

41. True (2 Kings 5:22).

42. Yes. Naaman gave Gehazi six thousand pieces of silver rather than the three thousand he asked for, plus the two changes of clothes that Gehazi requested (2 Kings 5:23).

43. False (2 Kings 5:26). Elisha rebuked him for his greed.

44. d. said that Gehazi and his family would always be plagued with leprosy (2 Kings 5:27). Elisha probably reacted this way because the servant's greed had left a bad mark on Elisha's prophetic ministry. The fact that Naaman was happy to pay handsomely to be rid of his leprosy shows how great a punishment Gehazi and his family would suffer.

A VISIT FROM THE QUEEN

1. The story of the queen's visit can be found in the Old Testament.

2. d. Sheba (1 Kings 10:1 and 2 Chronicles 9:1).

3. a. she had heard of his fame (1 Kings 10:1 and 2 Chronicles 9:1).

6. True (1 Kings 10:1 and 2 Chronicles 9:1).

7. d. unknown. Her questions are not recorded in the Bible. Some scholars believe they may have been puzzling riddles designed to stump Solomon.

8. a. wisdom and sacrifices to God (1 Kings 10:4-5 and 2 Chronicles 9:3-4).

9. c. riches, palace, food, and servants (1 Kings 10:4-5 and 2 Chronicles 9:3-4).

10. False. The queen told Solomon she was amazed that he possessed twice as much wisdom as she had been told (1 Kings 10:7 and 2 Chronicles 9:6).

11. True (1 Kings 10:9 and 2 Chronicles 9:8).

12. Because she was from a foreign land, it is assumed the Queen of Sheba worshipped pagan gods rather than the God of Israel. When she saw Solomon's riches and heard his wisdom, she considered him blessed by God, causing her to praise Him. Christians today are witnesses for Jesus Christ. However, Jesus asks us to live a life of love and forgiveness under his grace rather than displaying vast wealth.

14. The total is 49,950 pounds. This is about the same weight as 12 ½ Mercury Villager minivans.

NEHEMIAH BUILDS A WALL

1. The book of Nehemiah is found in the Old Testament.

2. As the title suggests, the book was written by Nehemiah.

4. c. suffering (Nehemiah 1:3).

5. False. The walls had been destroyed, which is why Nehemiah was called upon to undertake building the wall.

6. True (Nehemiah 1:11).

7. a. wept and prayed to God (Nehemiah 1:4-11).

8. b. cup bearer (Nehemiah 2:2). This was an important position that put Nehemiah in the king's presence every day.

9. b. looked sad (Nehemiah 2:3). Nehemiah had never before looked sad, so the king asked him if he was sick. Nehemiah told the king his people were unhappy.

10. c. go back and rebuild the city of Jerusalem (Nehemiah 2:5).

11. Yes, the king granted Nehemiah's request (Nehemiah 2:7).

12. True (Nehemiah 2:3).

14. b. his donkey (Nehemiah 2:12).

15. True (Nehemiah 2:19).

16. Nehemiah counted on God (Nehemiah 2:20).

18. d. the sheep gate (Nehemiah 3:1 and 3:32).

19. False. In fact, people tried to stop the work many times. Enemies made fun of the wall builders (Nehemiah 2:19 and 4:1-3); they threatened an attack (Nehemiah 4:7-23); enemies tried to distract Nehemiah from the project (Nehemiah 6:1-4); people tried to ruin Nehemiah's reputation (Nehemiah 6:5-9 and 10-14); finally, letters were sent to Nehemiah to scare him into stopping the project (Nehemiah 6:17-19).

20. False. He prayed to God, and the enemies' plans to sabotage the project were halted (Nehemiah 4:14-15).

22. a. they were too poor to feed their families (Nehemiah 5:2).

23. c. the rich Jews were taking advantage of their poor relatives (Nehemiah 5:7). They were forcing them to pay high taxes. They also loaned them money to be paid back with interest, a practice that was against the Jewish religion. Some people were so poor that they had to sell themselves into slavery (Nehemiah 5:4-6).

24. True (Nehemiah 5:12).

26. b. shook his sash (Nehemiah 5:13).

27. Yes (Nehemiah 5:13).

28. False: Nehemiah did not tax his people or buy property for himself (Nehemiah 5:15-16).

29. Nehemiah knew that the people already had enough burdens without him claiming a large amount of money and land for himself (Nehemiah 5:18). This is in contrast to the way the rich Jews were treating their relatives in Jerusalem.

30. The wall took fifty-two days to complete
    (Nehemiah 6:15).

LAMENTATIONS

1. The Book of Lamentations is found in the Old
   Testament after the book of Jeremiah.

2. a. being sorry about something.

4. d. the destruction of Jerusalem in 586 BC.

6. True (Lamentations 1).

7. b. anger (Lamentations 2).

8. True (Lamentations 3:57-58).

9. True (Lamentations 5).

HOSEA

2. The name of Hosea's wife was Gomer (Hosea 1:3).

3. Jezreel (Hosea 1:4), Jezreel (Hosea 1:5).

5. house of Israel (Hosea 1:6).

6. True (Hosea 1:9).

7. No. There would come a time when Israel would be loved again by God (Hosea 1:10-11).

8. False. She was unfaithful to Hosea, just as Israel was unfaithful to God (Hosea 2:2-13).

9. c. win Gomer back (Hosea 2:14-17).

10. Gomer's unfaithfulness to Hosea is like Israel's unfaithfulness to God because, just as a husband wants his wife to love him, God wanted Israel to love Him.

11. God says he will become close to Israel, and will show Israel great love. In return, Israel will love Him (Hosea 2:19-23).

12. False. He said they did not remember Him or accept His teachings (Hosea 4:6).

13. b. worshipping other gods (Hosea 4:10-13).

14. God was angry at Judah (Hosea 5:10).

15. a. invading and oppressing Israel (Hosea 5:10).

16. True (Hosea 5:15).

17. God says He wants love from His people (Hosea 6:5).

18. d. half-baked loaf of bread (Hosea 7:8). This means they rely too much on foreigners (verse 9) instead of God.

19. God says the nation of Israel is like a silly dove (Hosea 7:11).

20. d. flitting from place to place (Hosea 7:12). This means that the Israelites can not decide what to do. They go from one country to another, seeking help.

22. True (Hosea 8:1-14).

23. Returning to Egypt meant returning to a life of slavery. The story about how God released the Israelites from slavery in Egypt can be found in Exodus 1-14.

24. b. calves (Hosea 13:2).

25. True (Hosea 14:1).

26. d. forgive their sins (Hosea 14:2).

28. They promise not to worship other gods (Hosea 14:3).

29. a. a new life (Hosea 14:4-8).

30. John 3:16 says: For God so loved the world, that he gave his only begotten Son, that whosoever believeth in him should not perish, but have everlasting life (King James Version).

JOEL

2. Joel wrote the book of Joel.

3. a. the Old Testament, after Hosea.

4. b. prophet.

5. True.

6. b. locusts (Joel 1:4).

7. True (Joel 1:4). A plague of locusts had invaded the land.

8. b. repent of their sins (Joel 2:12).

9. True (Joel 2:18-19).

10. True (Joel 2:21-23).

11. The people should be glad because of what God had done for them. They will have plenty to eat and will never be hated again (Joel 2:25-27).

12. False. God will judge the nations in the Valley of Jehoshaphat (Joel 3:2).

14. d. Judah (Joel 3:19).

15. The Lord will live on Mount Zion (Joel 3:21).

MICAH

2. As its name suggests, Micah wrote the book of Micah.

3. a. Old Testament, after the book of Jonah.

4. True.

5. b. idolatry (Micah 1:5).

6. Micah said Samaria would lie in ruins (Micah 1:6).

7. d. walking naked and howling (Micah 1:8).

8. False (Micah 1:9).

9. The people did not like Micah's prophecy because they did not want to hear about being punished. They wanted to hear that they were good and they could do anything they wanted (Micah 2:6-11).

10. a. lie (Micah 2:11).

11. False. He said the rulers were evil (Micah 3:1).

13. True.

15. a. they thought the Lord was with them (Micah 3:11).

16. True (Micah 4:5).

17. This ruler is Jesus (Micah 5:2).

18. False: Bethlehem was a small town, yet it is the birth place of Jesus.

20. a. Assyria (Micah 5:6).

21. False. God wants us to have a relationship with Him (Micah 6:8).

22. False. Evil people will get no joy from their earthly treasures. The Lord hates for people to get things by being dishonest (6:9-16).

THE GOSPELS

1. The Bible has four Gospels: Matthew, Mark, Luke, and John.

2. a. first part of the New Testament.

3. A concordance is a list of words you can find in certain Bible verses. For instance, if you want to find out where the Bible talks about love, you can look up the word "love" in a concordance. The concordance should have a list of verses with the word "love" in them. Look in the back of your Bible. Does

it have a concordance? You can use it the next time you want to find a verse. The concordance in the back of your Bible will not be complete because a complete concordance would make your Bible too big to carry to church. A big book called an exhaustive concordance will list every verse and word, and might be a good study tool to help you learn even more about your Bible.

4. c. Matthew, Mark, Luke, and John.

5. a. the life and ministry of Jesus.

6. The red letters mean that those words were spoken by Jesus Himself. Many King James Version Bibles print Jesus' words in red. Some new versions do not.

7. b. the Acts of the Apostles and Revelation (Acts 1:4-5, 8-9, 9:4-6, 10-12, 15-16; 11:16; 18:9-10; 20:35; 22:7-8, 10, 18, 21; 23:11; 26:14-18, and Revelation 1:8, 11; 1:17-3:22; 22:7, 12-13, 16, 20).

8. False. Although Jesus is quoted in all four Gospels, He did not actually write any part of them.

10. b. collected taxes for Rome.

11. Matthew traced Jesus' lineage back to King David because he wanted to show us that Jesus is King. Jesus is worthy of our worship.

13. True.

14. Although it is not the longest Gospel, the book of Matthew is the Gospel with the greatest number of chapters.

The Birth of Jesus

1. True. The story of Jesus' birth is also found in Luke.

3. b. Joseph (Matthew 1:18).

5. An angel of the Lord first told Mary she would have a baby (Luke 1:28-33).

6. True (Luke 1:39-40).

7. True (Matthew 1:20).

9. Jesus was born in Bethlehem (Luke 2:5-7).

10. b. a census was being taken (Luke 2:1-3). A census is a count of how many people are living in a place at a certain time in history. The United States government takes a census of everyone in the country every ten years. Looking at old census records is one way to find out about your own ancestors.

11. False. King Herod was jealous of the new baby because Jesus was called King of the Jews (Matthew 2:1-3).

13. a. gold, frankincense, and myrrh (Matthew 2:11).

14. False. There was no room for them in the inn (Luke 2:7).

15. c. angels (Luke 2:8-14).

17. False. God warned them in a dream not to go back to King Herod. They returned to their country by another road (Matthew 2:12).

18. False. She had been told what to name Jesus (Luke 2:21).

19. a. Egypt (Matthew 2:13).

20. d. died (Matthew 2:14-15).

22. Nazarene (Matthew 2:23). This is in keeping with the word of the prophets about the Messiah.

24. c. it was required by Mosaic Law (Luke 2:24). The freedom we enjoy as Christians did not come about until after Jesus' ministry and resurrection.

25. Simeon (Luke 2:25). Upon seeing the baby, Simeon told Mary and Joseph that Jesus was the Messiah.

26. b. Jerusalem (Luke 2:22).

27. True. He was proclaimed the Messiah by Simeon, and also Anna the prophetess (Luke 2:22-38).

JESUS GROWS UP

2. True.

3. d. Nazareth (Luke 2:39).

4. c. Passover (Luke 2:45).

5. It took Mary and Joseph three days to find Jesus (Luke 2:45).

6. a. in the Temple, amazing the teachers with his wisdom (Luke 2:46).

7. True (Luke 2:49). He answered them, "How is it that you sought me? Wist ye not that I must be about my Father's business?" (King James Version). This means, "Why did you look for me? Didn't you know I was doing my Father's work?"

8. a. John the Baptist. Before John the Baptist was born, he jumped for joy upon hearing of Jesus' impending birth (Luke 1:41). He baptized Jesus (Matthew 3:13-17; Mark 1:9-11; Luke 3:21-22; John 1:31-34). Jesus spoke about John the Baptist after John's death (Matthew 11:12-19; Luke 7:19-35).

10. d. locusts and wild honey (Mark 1:6).

11. True (Matthew 3:11-12).

12. True (Mark 1:8).

13. c. was evil (Luke 3:19).

14. He was put into prison (Luke 3:20).

15. John the Baptist (Matthew 3:13-17; Mark 1:9-11; Luke 3:21-22; John 1:31-34).

16. d. a dove (Luke 3:21-22).

17. False. Instead, Jesus told Satan that people need more than bread. They also need God's word (Matthew 4:4).

18. c. Jesus was very hungry and wanted to eat because he had not eaten for forty days (Matthew 4:1-3). Satan thought Jesus' hunger would cause Him to give in to this temptation. Satan was mistaken.

20. If you think that Satan challenged Jesus in these ways to see whether Jesus was prideful, you are probably right. Pride is responsible for many sins. Satan often uses human pride in his tests. By telling Jesus He could prove He was God's son by performing miracles, Satan hoped Jesus' pride would cause Him to fail the tests. By resisting Satan, Jesus showed us that God is more important than our own pride.

21. True. Matthew 4:5-7.

22. a. all the world's kingdoms (Matthew 4:9).

23.   Angels helped Jesus after He was tempted by Satan.

25.   Jesus began his ministry in Galilee (Luke 4:14).

JESUS HEALS THE SICK

1.   a. the Gospels.

3.   False. He told the man not to tell anyone, but to go
         directly to the priest and offer the sacrifice
         required under Moses' law (Matthew 8:1-4).

4.   d. giving an order for him to be healed (Matthew 8:5-
         13 and Luke 7:1-10). Jesus healed the officer's ser-
         vant merely by ordering him to get well. This was
         unusual because Jesus did not even enter the
         officer's house to see or touch the servant.

6.   Jesus healed Peter's mother-in-law (Matthew 8:14-15).
         Peter is called Simon in Mark 1:30-31 and Luke 4:38-
         39, which also give account of this particular healing.

7.   b. touching her hand (Matthew 8:14-15, Mark 1:30-
         31, Luke 4:38-39).

9. True (Luke 4:41).

10. False. Jesus gave the demons an order not to speak, because He did not want them to tell who He was (Luke 4:41).

11. a. herd of pigs (Matthew 8:28-34, Mark 5:1-20, Luke 8:26-39).

12. b. were afraid (Mark 5:15, Luke 8:35).

13. True (Matthew 8:34, Mark 5:17, Luke 8:37).

14. After the man was healed, he wanted to go with Jesus (Mark 5:18, Luke 8:38).

15. True (Mark 5:19, Luke 8:39).

16. Yes (Mark 5:20).

17. a. cloak (Matthew 9:20, Mark 5:28, Luke 8:44).

18. d. faith (Matthew 9:22, Mark 5:34, Luke 8:48).

20. True (Matthew 9:23). In fact, preparations were already being made for her funeral.

21. sleeping (Matthew 9:24, Mark 5:39, Luke 8:52).

22. b. two blind men (Matthew 9:27-29).

23. Jesus told them not to tell anyone (Matthew 9:30).

24. No. Word of the healing spread everywhere
(Matthew 9:31).

LUKE TELLS US ABOUT JESUS

1. Luke's Gospel is the third book in the New
Testament.

3. The Acts of the Apostles is the fifth book in the New
Testament.

4. True.

5. The four Gospels are: Matthew, Mark, Luke, John.

6. True. You can read about them in the Gospels. Some
of them are recorded in Luke 4:31-5:26 and 6:6-19.

7. a. tax collectors and outcasts (Luke 5:30). Some religious leaders in Jesus' day did not understand why the Messiah would spend time with tax collectors and outcasts. In Jesus' day, tax collectors often kept much of the tax money for themselves and were thought to be stealing from others.

8. True (Luke 6:1-5). Some Pharisees were upset with Jesus' disciples for picking wheat to eat on the Sabbath. Jesus told them King David had fed his hungry troops rather than stick to a strict religious rule. It was hard for the Pharisees to argue with Jesus about this, since King David was a hero. Jesus' point was that people are more important than following rules.

9. c. a man with a paralyzed hand (Luke 6:6-10). Although Jesus knew He was being watched by enemies who were hoping He would break the Jewish law about the Sabbath, Jesus healed the man anyway. Jesus said it was lawful to do good on the Sabbath. Again, this showed how Jesus valued people more than rules.

10. False (Luke 6:11). Jesus' enemies were angry that he had broken the Jewish law.

11. a. follower.

12. Jesus' disciples are named in Luke 6:12-16. They are:
    Simon, whom he named Peter
    Andrew, Simon's brother
    James
    John
    Philip
    Bartholomew
    Matthew
    Thomas
    James son of Alphaeus
    Simon, who was called the Patriot (or the Zealot)
    Judas son of James
    Judas Iscariot, who became the traitor.

13. Soon after he chose his disciples, Jesus preached the Sermon on the Mount, also known as the Beatitudes (Luke 6:20-26).

14. False. Jesus said we should love our enemies (Luke 6:27).

16. The Golden Rule says to do unto others as you would have them do unto you. This means you should treat everyone else the same way you would like them to treat you.

17.   False (Luke 6:37-42). We should be careful about how we judge other people, because God will judge us by the same standards we use for others.

18.   a. washed his feet with her tears (Luke 7:36-37).

19.   d. said that Jesus shouldn't let a sinful woman touch him (Luke 7:39).

20.   True (Luke 7:47).

21.   Jesus said, "Thy sins are forgiven." and "Thy faith hath saved thee; go in peace" (Luke 7:48).

22.   False. Luke names several women who followed Jesus, including Mary Magdalene, Joanna, Susanna, and other unnamed women (Luke 8:1-3).

LUKE TELLS US WHAT JESUS SAID

1.   A parable is a lesson told in story form.

2.   d. his disciples could understand them, but not everyone else (Luke 8:10). Jesus did not want to share his knowledge with everyone, only those who truly wanted to follow him.

3. False. Jesus said that his family are those who hear and obey God (Luke 8:21). This does not mean we are not to love and honor our families, but that we are to be close to people who love the Lord, whether or not they are family members.

4. a. John the Baptist (Luke 9:7-9, 18, 20). John the Baptist was a cousin of Jesus whose ministry was legendary. Some people also thought that Jesus was Elijah or another prophet come back to life.

5. Resurrected means brought back to life from the dead.

6. True (Luke 9:21-22).

9. d. Moses and Elijah (Luke 9:31). This was amazing because both Moses and Elijah had long been dead.

10. Jesus' visitors talked to him about how he would soon fulfill God's plan for him (Luke 9:31).

12. b. were afraid and told no one (Luke 9:36).

13. True (Luke 9:46).

14. Jesus said that the person who is the least important on earth is the most important person in heaven. This is an important teaching of Jesus because it is the opposite of what the world teaches and it even goes against our own human nature. Rather than looking to be the most important person in the world, it is better for us to put Jesus first.

15. a. told him to stop (Luke 9:49). They were upset because he was not part of their group.

16. Jesus said, "Forbid him not; for he that is not against us is for us." (Luke 9:50). This means Jesus welcomes all who love Him, not just people who belong to a certain group.

18. False. The Samaritan village did not want Jesus to come through there because he was on his way to Jerusalem. James and John asked Jesus if he wanted them to command fire to come from heaven to destroy the village (Luke 9:54).

19. c. not to be unforgiving toward the citizens of the town. He said, "Ye know not what manner of spirit ye are of; For the Son of man is not come to destroy men's lives, but to save them" (Luke 9:55-56, King James Version). This means he told the disciples not to be so mean-spirited. Jesus wants to save us.

20. False. Jesus and the disciples went another way (Luke 9:56).

22. d. nothing (Luke 10:4).

23. The workers would be taken care of by the people in each town. They were told to go to a house and greet the people living there with peace. Those people were to give them food and shelter during their stay in the town.

24. a. lambs among wolves (Luke 10:3).

25. True (Luke 10:17).

THE PRODIGAL SON

1. Jesus told the story of the prodigal son.

2. You can find the story of the prodigal son in Luke 15:11-32.

3. False.

4. The word "prodigal" means recklessly extravagant; lavish.

5. The wealthy man had two sons (Luke 15:11).

6. a. give him his share of his inheritance (Luke 15:12).

7. b. property that is passed on when someone dies.

8. True (Luke 15:11-13).

9. c. wasted his money (Luke 15:13).

10. d. tending pigs (Luke 15:15).

12. False. The father ran to the son, hugged him, and kissed him (Luke 15:20).

13. d. a ring, a robe, and shoes (Luke 15:22).

14. True (Luke 15:23-24).

15. False. He begged the older brother to join the party (Luke 15:28).

16. d. was angry (Luke 15:28).

17. He was upset because he had not been rewarded with a party, even though he had been faithful and had never strayed from the father (Luke 29-30).

18. c. "Everything I have is yours and we are close" (Luke 15: 31).

19. True (Luke 15:32). The younger brother had been lost, but was found. He had been dead, but was alive.

THE GOOD SAMARITAN

1. You can find the story of the Good Samaritan in Luke 10:25-37.

2. False: The parable of the Good Samaritan can be found only in Luke.

4. c. a story that teaches a lesson.

5. d. "Who is my neighbor?" (Luke 10:29).

6. a. a lawyer (Luke 10:25).

7. c. had been beaten and robbed (Luke 10:30).

8. False (Luke 10:31-32).

9. The man was on his way from Jerusalem to Jericho (Luke 10:30).

10. The Samaritan stopped to help the injured man (Luke 10:33).

13. c. oil and wine (Luke 10:34).

14. True (Luke 10:35).

15. c. an inn (Luke 10:34).

16. The Samaritan give the innkeeper two denarii (Luke 10:35).

18. True. The lawyer said the neighbor was the person who showed mercy (Luke 10:36).

19. The Samaritan acted as a neighbor.

20. d. "Go and do likewise" (Luke 10:37). This means we should be kind to people in need whether or not they belong to our group.

JESUS' RESURRECTION

1. True. Although all four Gospels don't talk about everything that happened to Jesus, all do record His resurrection (Matthew 28:1-15; Mark 16:1-11; Luke 24: 1-12; John 20:1-18).

2. Matthew 28:1 names Mary Magdalene, Mary the mother of James, and Salome. There were other unnamed women. Luke 24:10 names Joanna.

3. a. an angel of the Lord (Matthew 28:2).

4. c. "Fear not, for Jesus has risen" (Matthew 28:5-6). Note: An earthquake had already happened when the angel rolled away the stone (Matthew 28:2).

5. False (Luke 24:11). They thought the women were telling idle tales.

6. Jesus' disciples Peter and John went to the grave. The King James Version refers to John as "the other disciple whom Jesus loved" (John 20:2-4).

7. True (John 20:11-18).

8. c. "Peace be unto you" (John 20:19).

9. c. wanted to reassure them (John 20:19). They were hiding because they feared they would be killed for following Jesus.

The Lord's Prayer

2. The Lord's Prayer appears in both Luke and Matthew. The version from Matthew 6:9-13 is quoted here from the King James Version because it is the more complete of the two:

> Our Father, who art in heaven, Hallowed by thy name. Thy Kingdom come. Thy will be done in earth, as it is in heaven. Give us this day our daily bread. And forgive us our debts as we forgive our debtors. And lead us not into temptation, but deliver us from evil. For thine is the kingdom, and the power, and the glory, forever and ever. Amen.

3. a. one of them had asked him to teach them how to pray (Luke 11:1).

4. God is in heaven.

5. He means that we should respect, honor, and revere God's holy name.

7. True.

8. True (Matthew 6:5).

9. A hypocrite is a person who acts like someone good in public but does evil things when no one else is watching.

11. False. The Lord's Prayer is a model for us to go by. However, sharing our own concerns with God helps us to become closer to Him. God loves you and He wants to hear about your cares. He also likes for you to thank Him for his goodness.

13. This prayer is named The Lord's Prayer because Jesus taught it to us.

14. d. God will forgive us when we forgive others (Matthew 6:14-15).

15. False. Those who pray in the open to get praise already have their reward (Matthew 6:16).

PAUL SPEAKS ABOUT LOVE

1. The Apostle Paul wrote 1 Corinthians.

2. b. members of the church at Corinth. Paul's letters to them gave advice on how they should live as Christians.

4. False. Without love, any speech is just a lot of noise (I Corinthians 13:1).

5. d. none of the above. You must have love (I Corinthians 13:2-3).

6. d. proud (I Corinthians 13:4). This means you will let the person you love be first, or the most important.

7. This means if you love someone, it will take a lot to make you mad at that person.

8. False (I Corinthians 13:8-9).

9. Love is the greatest (I Corinthians 13:13).

THE FRUIT OF THE SPIRIT

1. c. a set of attitudes you'll have if you love God.

2. We can learn about the fruit of the Spirit in Galatians 5:22-26.

179

3. The apostle Paul told us about the fruit of the Spirit.

4. a. members of a group of churches in Galatia.

6. Paul speaks of love in 1 Corinthians 13.

7. b. happiness in the Lord.

9. c. you can forgive other people when they sin against you.

11. True (Galatians 5:22).

12. False. No matter what, a person of faith always believes in God (Hebrews 11:1).

13. c. strong, but kind to others.

14. d. controlling yourself and not going to the extreme.

15. False. He wanted to show that Christian conduct is more important than following the law (Galatians 5:18).

16. d. don't think about their bodies as much as they think about living for Christ (Galatians 5:25).

17. a. we obey Christ (Galatians 5:25).

18. False. Christians should not seek others' possessions (Galatians 5:26).

19. There are many good reasons to obey Christ. In this passage, Paul is showing us how we will act if we are obedient. Loving others is a good way to be an ambassador for Christ.

20. The nine elements of the fruit of the Spirit are love, joy, peace, long-suffering, gentleness, goodness, faith, meekness, and temperance.

1 PETER

1. a. Peter.

2. True.

3. b. is named first in every list of the apostles in the Bible. These lists are found in Matthew 10:2-4, Mark 3:13-19, Luke 6:12-16 and Acts 1:13-14.

4. b. persecuted Christians (1 Peter 1:1).

5. d. eternal life. The Christian looks forward to living with God in heaven rather than having lots of things here.

6. True (1 Peter 1:14). Jesus' teachings go against the world's system of greed and materialism. Instead of encouraging us to get more stuff, he tells us God will provide our needs. When we trust God, there is no need to be greedy or to wish we had more than someone else.

7. "Redeemed" means saved. Those who accept Jesus' gift of salvation are saved and forgiven for their sins.

8. a. Jesus (1 Peter 1:7). Jesus redeemed us when He was crucified on the cross.

9. Thou shalt not covet (Exodus 20:17). We should not be jealous of other people's things or accomplishments, but be happy for them in their success. When you are jealous of someone, think about everything God has done for you.

10. The warning to put aside evil speaking might remind us of the commandment not to bear false witness against our neighbor, or not to tell lies (Exodus 20:16).

11. a. newborn babes (1 Peter 2:2). This means we should desire the pure milk of the word, which is the word of God.

12. d. make Christians grow (1 Peter 2:2). The more we read the Bible, the more we learn about Jesus and the Christian faith.

13. c. living stones (1 Peter 2:5).

14. True (1 Peter 2:5).

16. True (1 Peter 2:7). This means Jesus is the foundation of our faith.

17. This means people who don't want to obey Jesus will trip over his word and find it insulting and offensive.

18. True (1 Peter 2:11-12). We are ambassadors for Christ. Our conduct should cause unbelievers to praise the Lord.

19. A sojourner is a guest. We are guests in this world, because our true home is in heaven with the Lord. We can enjoy God's awesome creation while we live here.

20. False (1 Peter 2:11). He means Christians are not at home in this world.

21. b. obey the laws of their nations (1 Peter 2:13). If we obey the law, no one can say we think we are above the law. Christians are obligated to be good citizens.

22. False (1 Peter 2:18). We are to forgive others.

23. a. remember how Jesus trusted God (1 Peter 2:23-24). Jesus did not insult people who insulted him. He trusted God.

24. c. lost sheep (1 Peter 2:25). This means they were sinners who had gotten away from God.

25. The three parables are about the lost sheep (Matthew 18:12-14 and Luke 15:3-7); the lost son (Luke 15:11-32); and the lost coin (Luke 15:8-10).

26. Psalm 23 refers to Jesus as a shepherd.

27. "Submit" means to comply, to obey, or to go along with someone.

28. False (1 Peter 3:1). The wife should submit to her husband, even if he does not obey Christ. This does not mean the wife is a slave to the husband or that she should be mistreated, but that she should honor her marriage vows. Because the Christian church was just beginning to take hold in the world at the time Peter wrote this letter, some women who proclaimed Christ were already married to men who practiced pagan religions. By giving this instruction, Peter was discouraging these women from divorce.

30. False (1 Peter 3:3-4). Beauty from within is precious to God.

31. d. honor their wives (1 Peter 3:7).

32. a. not as strong physically as her husband (1 Peter 3:7). This does not mean the woman is not as good as the man or inferior to him; it just means that she is not as muscular or as strong in the body. He was encouraging husbands to look out for their wives' best interests and to protect them.

33. True (1 Peter 3:7).

34. True (1 Peter 3:14). Peter wrote this to encourage Christians who were suffering just for being Christians. Some important people in the government did not like Christians, and they tried to make their lives difficult. Sometimes people were even killed for being Christians.

35. b. meekness (1 Peter 3:15-16).

36. The Sermon on the Mount, where he preached the Beatitudes (Matthew 5:1-12 and Luke 6:20-26).

38. d. when you love people, you can forget about their sins (1 Peter 4:8). It is easier to forgive someone you love than someone you hate.

39. True (1 Peter 4:15).

40. a. be busybodies.

41. Our earthly shepherds in the church today are elders of the church, or pastors (1 Peter 5:1).

42. b. elders (1 Peter 5:5).

43. God wants us to respect our parents. They can teach us a lot about life and how to be Christians.

44. The devil is the enemy of Christians (I Peter 5:8).

45. Amen is the last word in I Peter (I Peter 5:14).

2 PETER

1. We know that Peter is the author because he tells us
   in 2 Peter 1:1.

3. a. Christians in Asia Minor (2 Peter 1:1).

4. It is important to study all sixty-six books of the
   Bible. Peter's letters are important because they give
   us instructions on how to live as Christians.

5. True (2 Peter 1:3-4).

6. The traits a Christian should have are: faith, virtue,
   knowledge, self-control, perseverance, godliness,
   brotherly kindness, and love (2 Peter 1:5-7). Can you
   think of someone who is like this? Think about how
   Christians can display these characteristics in real life.

8. c. die (2 Peter 1:14). The New King James Version calls the tabernacle a tent. This is symbolic of how short life on earth is in comparison to eternal life with God. Few people live in a tent all their lives on earth. Likewise, we live in our bodies for a time until we go and live with God in heaven.

9. True (2 Peter 1:16-18).

10. False. False prophets will be punished (2 Peter 2:12-13).

11. d. all of the above (2 Peter 2:1-3).

12. a. a talking donkey (2 Peter 2:15).

13. Peter means that people who are not truly devoted to the Lord may seem to be faithful for awhile, but will sooner or later return to their wicked ways.

14. b. as a thief in the night (2 Peter 3:10). This means it will be unexpected. Do not listen to anyone who claims to know the exact day the Lord will return. Not even Jesus knows this day (Matthew 24:36).

15. True. We must stay faithful to God's word (2 Peter 3:17).

AWESOME BOOKS FOR KIDS!

The Young Reader's Christian Library
Action, Adventure, and Fun Reading!

This series for young readers ages eight to twelve is action
packed, fast-paced, and Christ-centered! With exciting illustra
tions on every other page following the text, these books ar
hard for kids to put down! Over 100 illustrations per book. Al
books are paperbound. The unique size (4 1/8" x 5 3/8") make
these books easy to take anywhere!

A Great Selection to Satisfy All Kids!

Abraham Lincoln	*Heidi*	*Pocahontas*
Ben-Hur	*Hudson Taylor*	*Pollyanna*
Billy Graham	*In His Steps*	*Prudence of Plymouth*
Billy Sunday	*Jesus*	*Plantation*
Christopher	*Jim Elliot*	*Robinson Crusoe*
Columbus	*Joseph*	*Roger Williams*
Corrie ten Boom	*Little Women*	*Ruth*
Daniel	*Lydia*	*Samuel Morris*
David Brainerd	*Miriam*	*The Swiss Family*
David Livingstone	*Moses*	*Robinson*
Deborah	*Paul*	*Thunder in the*
Elijah	*Peter*	*Valley*
Esther	*The Pilgrim's*	*Wagons West*
Florence Nightingale	*Progress*	

Available wherever books are sold.

Or order from: Barbour Publishing, Inc., P.O. Box 719
Uhrichsville, Ohio 44683
http://www.barbourbooks.com

$2.50 each retail, plus $1.00 for postage and handling per order.
Prices subject to change without notice.